John Preston Young

The Seventh Tennessee Cavalry

A History

John Preston Young

The Seventh Tennessee Cavalry
A History

ISBN/EAN: 9783337812621

Printed in Europe, USA, Canada, Australia, Japan

Cover: Foto ©ninafisch / pixelio.de

More available books at **www.hansebooks.com**

THE

SEVENTH TENNESSEE CAVALRY.

CONFEDERATE.

A HISTORY.

BY J. P. YOUNG,
Of Company A.

Printed for the Author.
Publishing House of the M. E. Church, South.
Barbee & Smith, Agents, Nashville, Tenn.
1890.

DEDICATION.

To My Comrades Who Survive, and to the Memory of Those Who Fell in Battle Upholding the Banner of One of the Proudest of Confederate Cavalry Organizations in a Cause They Loved,
THIS LITTLE VOLUME IS AFFECTIONATELY DEDICATED.

CONTENTS.

CHAPTER I.

The First Company—Calvary Organizations in West Tennessee—Gen. N. B. Forrest Enlists as a Private—Logwood's Battalion Organized—First Brush with the Enemy—At the Battle of Belmont—The Surprise at Union City—First Regimental Organization—The Charge at Lockridge Mills—First Regimental Reorganization and Roster of Officers.................................... 7

CHAPTER II.

Soldiers in Earnest—Capturing a Guarded Train—Severe Fighting at Bolivar, Medon, and Britton's Lane—A Reverse at Coldwater—The Charge at Davis's Bridge—Battle of Corinth—The Shooting of Captain Hill—A Stampede at Old Lamar—Covering the Retreat—The Fight at Coffeeville—Capture of Holly Springs—Companies B and A Detached—Death of Chaplain Crouch—The Affair at Hernando—Attack on Collierville—Escape of Gen. Sherman. 39

CHAPTER III.

Under Gen. Forrest—Assigned to the Fourth Brigade—Affair at Okolona—Battle of Prairie Mound—Death of Col. Forrest—Repulse of the Federal Onset—The March to West Tennessee—Capture of Union City—The Ruse of Col. Duckworth—Under Gen. Rucker—Battle of Tishomingo Creek—Lieut.-Col. Taylor's Charge—The Fight for Possession of the Ticket—Death of Adjt. Pope—Rout of the Enemy—The A. J. Smith Raid—Battle of Harrisburg—The Regiment's Charge on the Works—Frightful Slaughter of the Men—Rescuing the Flag—Death of Capt. Statler—The Pursuit—Lieut.-Col. Taylor Takes Command.. 74

CHAPTER IV.

Again Off for Tennessee—Capture of Athens—Rich Spoils of War—Col. Taylor Wounded—Assault on Pulaski—The March to Columbia—Capture of Block-houses—Retreat from Tennessee—The Ruse at Newport Ferry—A Council of War—All Safely Across—The Johnsonville Raid—Capture of the Gun-boats—Service as Horse Marines—Destruction of Stores at Johnsonville—A Novel Scheme to Shoe the Horses—Hood's March to Nashville—Driving the Enemy's Cavalry—Assaults on Mount Carmel and Spring Hill—The Struggle at Franklin—Before Nashville—Deadly Conflict with the Enemy's Right Wing—Col. Taylor Saves the Regiment—The Fighting at Harpeth River and Richland Creek—Hardships of the Winter Retreat—Recrossing the Tennessee—Relief for the Starving Horses.................................... 102

CHAPTER V.

Temporary Consolidation—The Regiment Furloughed—A Rush for Home—Return of the Men to Camp—The Regiment in Convention—Patriotic Resolutions—The Wilson Raid—March to Alabama—Conflicts at Scottsville and Centerville—The Last Gun—Announcement of the Surrender—Grief of the Men—Dividing the Old Flag—A Sad Farewell... 130

CHAPTER VI.

Detached Service of Company A under Gen. Jackson....... 140

ROLL... 152

The Seventh Tennessee Cavalry.

CHAPTER I.

The First Company—Cavalry Organizations in West Tennessee—Gen. N. B. Forrest Enlists as a Private—Logwood's Battalion Organized—First Brush with the Enemy—At the Battle of Belmont—The Surprise at Union City—First Regimental Organization—The Charge at Lockridge Mills—First Regimental Reorganization and Roster of Officers.

In May, 1861, the leaven of revolution was working with vehement energy in West Tennessee. The masses were thoroughly aroused. There was but one impulse, one sentiment, among the people, and that was resistance to coercion at whatever cost. In great part opposed to secession from the old Union, and not yet wedded to the principles of an independent self-government for the Southern States, already asserted farther South; yet with a unanimity of purpose and action rarely if ever equaled in former revolutions, the masses of the people—men and women—prepared for the impending conflict. Armed and uniformed men were to be seen on every side;

white tents dotted the fields and hill-sides; committees of ladies worked day and night upon the gray jackets, or solicited blankets at the farm-houses "for the boys in camp;" and the measured tread of companies, battalions, and regiments could be heard throughout the land. Whatever may now be thought of the wisdom of the great upheaval, no one at this day can question the sincerity or self-sacrificing devotion of the participants. Amid these stormy scenes the senior company of the historical Seventh Tennessee Cavalry Regiment, not the least famous of the splendid mounted organizations which afterward went to make up "Forrest's Cavalry," was sworn into the service of the State of Tennessee on May 16, 1861, for twelve months, and christened "Memphis Light Dragoons." The company had been organized the previous year, under an act of incorporation by the Tennessee Legislature, as a military company, and at the date of enlistment was officered as follows

  Captain, Thomas H. Logwood;
  First Lieutenant, Thomas Howard;
  Second Lieutenant, William F Taylor;
  Third Lieutenant, E. B. Trezevant.
  On May 31, 1861, "Hill's Cavalry," of Tip-

ton County, was organized at Mason's Depot, and mustered into the State service as twelve months men. It was officered as follows:

Captain, C. H. Hill;
First Lieutenant, F A. Claiborne;
Second Lieutenant, R. A. Field;
Third Lieutenant, J U Green.

This was afterward Company B.

On May ——, 1861, the "Marion Foxes," afterward styled the "Shelby Light Dragoons," was organized at Memphis, as follows:

Captain, John G Ballentyne;
First Lieutenant, W B. Maxwell;
Second Lieutenant, Kenneth Garrett;
Third Lieutenant, Martin S. Armstrong.

This was subsequently Company C. S. P. Bassett was the second captain, and was wounded and disabled at Medon August 31, 1862. Second Lieutenant John Allbright was also killed at Medon, Tenn.

About June 14, 1861, the "Tennessee Mounted Rifles" was mustered into service at Memphis, by Captain Josiah S. White. The other officers were:

First Lieutenant, William Montgomery;
Second Lieutenant, A. R. Moore;
Third Lieutenant, William Hall.

It was constituted Company D, in the first battalion organization, on September 7, 1861. In this company N B. Forrest, afterward Lieutenant-general of Cavalry, was enrolled as a private soldier June 14, 1861.

Company D, as lettered at the reorganization of the regiment, June 10, 1862, was organized at Brownsville, in Haywood County, (the first company), in April, 1861. The officers were:

Captain, R. W Haywood;

First Lieutenant, L. H. Johnson;

Second Lieutenant, J W. Jones;

Third Lieutenant, J M. Shaw

Company E was organized at Bolivar, in Hardeman County, in the spring of 1861. The first officers were as follows:

Captain, J J Neely;

First Lieutenant, T G. Patrick;

Second Lieutenant, Leon Bills;

Brevet Second Lieutenant, W W McCauley

Company F, or the "Forked Deer Rangers," enlisted in Haywood County, and was mustered into the service of the Confederate States at Camp Beauregard, Ky., November 4, 1861, under

Captain, C. C. Clay;

First Lieutenant, H. G. Winburn;
Second Lieutenant, C. A. Jones;
Brevet Second Lieutenant, J. E. Gregory.

Company G was organized at Paris, Tenn., and was sworn into service November 13, 1861, with these officers, to wit:

Captain, J G. Stocks,
First Lieutenant, F F. Aden;
Second Lieutenant, J J Blake;
Brevet Second Lieutenant, Benjamin Diggs.

Company H was organized at Dresden, Tenn., in the autumn of 1861, and was constituted as follows:

Captain, H. C. McCutchen;
First Lieutenant, J A. Jenkins;
Second Lieutenant, James Williams;
Brevet Second Lieutenant, E. T. Hollis.

Company I was mustered into service in Tipton County in 1862 by

Captain, Lafayette Hill;
First Lieutenant, John T. Douglass;
Second Lieutenant, Philip A. Fisher;
Brevet Second Lieutenant, Henry D. Smith.

Company K was organized in Shelby and Fayette Counties, with

Captain, Samuel F Taylor;

First Lieutenant. William F Broadnax;
Second Lieutenant, J J Mullins;
Brevet Second Lieutenant, W L. Burleson.

This company, late in the war, was very much diminished, and consolidated with Company C and others; and a company under Captain James A. Anderson, from Ballentyne's Battalion, took its place as Company K, at Verona, Miss., in February, 1865, with the following officers:

Captain, James A. Anderson;
First Lieutenant, J. S. Hiller;
Second Lieutenant, John Trent;
Brevet Second Lieutenant, E. R. Scruggs.

Company L was enlisted at Brownsville, Tenn., in April, 1862, and was organized May 12, 1862, with

Captain, James A. Taylor;
First Lieutenant, Alexander Duckworth;
Second Lieutenant, A. Austin;
Brevet Second Lieutenant, Frank Pugh.

Company M was enlisted and sworn into service in the spring of 1862, in Haywood and Lauderdale Counties, and elected the following officers:

Captain, James G. Haywood;
First Lieutenant, J M. Shaw;

Second Lieutenant, Benjamin T. Davis;
Brevet Second Lieutenant, William H. Moore.

These companies were composed entirely of volunteers, and the regiment into which they were finally merged never contained a conscript on the rolls. Their tender of service was in all cases prompted entirely by patriotism.

A complete roster of the officers and privates of these companies will be given on a subsequent page, with a list of casualties, promotions, etc., annexed.

It is impracticable in this short space to give a detailed account of the movements and adventures of these companies between the dates of their enlistment and the date of their enrollment in Logwood's Battalion, or subsequently in the Seventh Tennessee Cavalry They were not generally important.

Company A, after enlistment in the State service, went at once to Fort Randolph, Tenn., and reported for duty to Brig.-Gen. John L. T Sneed. Some weeks later it was ordered to accompany Gen. Pillow in his expedition to New Madrid, Mo.; and afterward, during the summer, was marched to

Columbus, Ky., under Gen. Polk. It remained there, doing picket duty, until September 7, when it became the senior Company A of Logwood's Battalion. The company was finely drilled, mounted, and equipped, and presented a martial appearance.

Company B, or "Hill's Cavalry," after its organization at Mason Depot, May 31, 1861, marched to Clopton Camp-ground, about six miles off, and remained there, encamped and drilling, until late in the summer, when they were ordered to Columbus, Ky. Here, on September 7, they became part of Logwood's Battalion, the nucleus of the Seventh Tennessee. In March, 1862, at Union City, the company elected J P Russell, Captain; H. T Sale, First Lieutenant; P T. Wynn, Second Lieutenant; and I. N Stinson, Brevet Second Lieutenant. This was at the date of the first organization of the regiment.

Company C was organized soon after Company A, and went into camp at the old fair-grounds, near Memphis, where they were drilled and tutored as soldiers until late in the summer, when they were ordered to Columbus, Ky., and became part of Logwood's Battalion. This company was well mounted, but poorly equipped, and armed with shotguns and pistols, their uniforms consisting of red shirts, without coats. Their drill, however, was very fine.

Company D (White's) has a history almost identical with Company A, from its enlistment in June, 1861, to its enrollment in the First Regiment in March, 1862, and it need not be here repeated.

Company D (Haywood's), after organization in April, 1861, remained at Brownsville until May 23, 1861, at which date it was mustered into the service of the State, at Jackson, as twelve months men, by Col. A. W. Campbell. H. J Livingston was made third lieutenant, *vice* J M. Shaw, resigned; and W L. Duckworth became second lieutenant shortly after, *vice* J. W Jones, resigned. It remained here until about the middle of July, when it was ordered to Fort Wright, at Randolph, and soon after joined Gen. Pillow's expedition from New Madrid into Missouri. While in Missouri Lieut. Johnson resigned, and Lieut. Duckworth became first lieutenant; Lieut. Livingston, second lieutenant; and James Bond, third lieutenant. Moving to Columbus, Ky., late in the summer, the company was, on September 7, by General Order No. 19, organized as part of Logwood's

Battalion; and on October 24, 1861, by Order No. 13 (First Division, Western Department), was detailed to serve with Gen. ——, Third Division, and was in a skirmish at Blandsville, Ky., in the fall of 1861. It remained at Camp Beauregard during the winter on outpost duty; and was ordered, about March 1, 1862, to Island 10, near which place it remained during the siege of the island. The company went thence, by order of Gen. McCown, to Fort Pillow; and soon after the battle of Shiloh, on April 7, 1861, was ordered to report to Col. Jackso at Trenton, and joined him about the middle of April, when it became part of the First Tennessee Regiment (Seventh), under the first organization by Col. Jackson.

Company E, after its enrollment at Bolivar in the early spring of 1861, marched to Jackson; thence to Randolph, and on to Columbus, Ky., where on September 7, by General Order No. 19, it became part of Logwood's Battalion; and on October 24, 1861, by General Order No. 13, the company was with Haywood's Company D detached to serve with the Third Division of Infantry At the end of March, 1862, it became part of the first or temporary organization of the

First Tennessee (Seventh), under Col. Jackson. The succeeding officers, in their order, were: W. J Tate and J. P Statler, Captains; and Fisk Weaver, T. P Harris, Lee Ruffin, and William Mashburn, Lieutenants.

The remaining companies, between the dates of their enlistment and organization (from November, 1861, to May, 1862) and their enrollment into the regiment, had no adventures of moment or interest, and commenced their fighting career as members of the First (afterward Seventh) Tennessee Cavalry

Four of the above companies—A, B, C, and D, or White's company—were engaged in outpost duty and in short scouting operations at Randolph, and afterward at Columbus, Ky., and the surrounding country, during July and August, 1861. On September 7 Gen. Polk, moved by the exigences of the service, issued General Order No. 19, at Columbus, directing the organization of a battalion out of the cavalry companies of Logwood, White, Neely, Haywood, Hill, and Ballentyne, the "Tennessee Troopers," and Bowie's and Faulkner's Alabama companies. The order contained this clause: "The election of field officers of the Tennessee Battalion having been suspended by appeal, and the necessities of the public service demanding battalion organization, the organization becomes a necessity " ("Rebel. Records," 3, p. 699.)

The election resulted in the choice of Capt. Thomas H. Logwood, of Company A, to be Lieutenant-Colonel; Capt. C. H. Hill, of Company B, as Major; and Private John W Somervell, of Company B, as Adjutant. The new organization was styled "Logwood's Battalion," being the Sixth Battalion of Tennessee Cavalry By reason of these promotions Lieut. W F Taylor became captain of Company A, and Lieut. J U Green, captain of Company B.

On September ——, 1861, the battalion commenced its fighting career, a small detachment being for the first time under fire. While engaged in the daily scout toward Elliott's Mills, on Mayfield Creek, Kentucky— a duty performed with such clock-like regularity by a detachment, over the same road, that it gave the enemy every opportunity to capture it—a squadron of ten men of Company C, under Sergeant Griffin, were fired upon from an ambuscade on the bluff, overhanging a ravine or road cut leading to the creek through a corn-field, into which they had unguardedly ridden. Being fresh men, unaccustomed to warfare, and having their guns strapped to their saddles for convenience of carriage, they imagined the enemy to be in large force; and, observing a line of men across the road in front who ordered them to surrender, they stampeded gallantly to the rear, smelling their first powder and losing one hat. The enemy, being an infantry picket of ten men of the Seventh Iowa Regiment, of course did not pursue, and the stampede halted a short distance rearward, except Private May, who did not pull rein until in camp. As an evidence of the doubtful efficiency of these early scouting parties on both sides, we find them severally reporting their antagonists' forces at about one hundred and fifty men. But they were not long in acquiring soldiership of a higher order.

On September 22, 1861, the battalion, by order of Gen. Polk, moved on Elliott's Mills, a hamlet on Mayfield Creek, Kentucky, ten miles from Columbus, to ascertain the enemy's strength at that point. The battalion charged in column into the midst of the enemy's encampment, and finding them strong in force, drew out and retired without loss.

The enemy lost one killed and five wounded in the skirmish.

Soon after (October ——, 1861) the battalion was for a third time brought under fire, near Paducah, Ky., and this time with severe loss. Lieut.-Col. Logwood moved at night, with Companies A and C, to the immediate vicinity of Paducah, and made an attack upon the enemy's pickets in the dark. This questionable movement resulted in the loss of Private Ed Gallagher, of Company C, who was instantly killed by the fire, probably, of our own men, and the wounding of Privates Holmes and Fleming, of Company A. The attack inflicted no loss, according to the Federal reports, on the enemy, though Lieut.-Col. Logwood reported killing and capturing their entire outpost. The two companies retired at once to their original positions, bringing off their dead and wounded. This was the first loss inflicted on the battalion after its formation.

On December 24, 1861, the battalion was attached, by General Order No. 13 (First Division, Western Department), to Gen. Pillow's First Division; and by the same order Haywood's Company D and Neely's Company E were detached to serve with the

Third Division, and Bowie's and Faulkner's Alabama companies to the Fourth Division, leaving only Companies A (Taylor's), B (Hill's), C (Ballentyne's), and D (White's), in the battalion. ("Rebel. Records," 3, p. 723.) Privates Gus Benson and J T. Hunt, of Company B, were both attacked with camp measles in the autumn of 1861, from which Benson died and Hunt was so broken in health as to incapacitate him for service.

On November 7, 1861, was fought the battle of Belmont, Mo., opposite Columbus, Ky., and Company A was ordered across the river, under Lieut.-Col. Logwood, to render such assistance as cavalry could in that combat. Once across, they were placed on the left of the army, under—or rather in conjunction with—Lieut.-Col. J H. Miller, commanding a battalion of Mississippi cavalry, including the Bolivar Troop and Thompson's Cavalry Reaching the field after the first onset of the enemy, the Tennessee troopers had but little part in this combat, other than skirmishing, but were treated for the first time to a view of the grand tactics of battle, though without loss other than a few horses. They were, however, made the victims of a prolix and stilted report of their commander,

Lieut.-Col. Miller, who consumed many pages of manuscript in narrating what his cavalry *did not do* in that noted battle. ("Rebel. Records," 3, 350.) White's Company D was carried over late in the day, as an escort, by Gen. Polk, and took but little part in the affair. Private Ed Gaylor, of Company C, failing to get leave to accompany the detachment across the river, evaded his commander and went over with a command of infantry— an act of enthusiasm which cost him his life, he being killed on the field.

During December and January the battalion was actively engaged in scouting and other duties, but in January encamped at Camp Desha, Moscow, Ky.

About February 3 a scouting party was sent out from Camp Desha toward the Tennessee River, under Col. Miller, along with which was Company B, Capt. J U Green, and Company G, Capt. J G Stocks. They moved to Paris and thence to the railroad bridge at Danville, where they found that the enemy had taken to their boats, and the gun-boats showing their teeth by opening their ports, the gallant horse soldiers retired out of range and returned to camp near Paris. They went soon after on a scout north-east of Paris, and finding the enemy's pickets drove them in on the main body Col. Miller, suspecting a ruse, sent Capt. Stocks's company forward to locate the enemy The captain, on ascending a high hill with his company, saw the ambuscade and also a battalion of Federals endeavoring to get in his rear. He at once opened fire on them and withdrew in haste, losing three men wounded and one captured. The command then returned to Camp Desha, reaching there on the 16th of February About February 19, 1862, the battalion made a winter's march to old Camp Beauregard, destroying the railroad from five miles south of Mayfield, Ky., to Fulton Station. They also burned Camp Beauregard after removing a large amount of commissary stores. (Logwood's report, " Reb. Records," 7, 897) On March 4 the battalion was still at Camp Desha, and was reported by its commander as 180 strong. March 7 the battalion burned bridges over Little Obion, also burned Camp Desha, and on the 8th of March moved to Union City, where Col. Logwood, who had received a commission to raise a regiment of lancers, turned the battalion over to Maj. C. H. Hill on the same day

March 15 it was ordered by Gen. Beauregard to March to Fort Pillow

Toward the close of the month the following companies. viz.: A. B, C. D (White's), E. F. G. H. and I, were assembled at Union City to be organized in a regiment of Confederate troops under Col. William H. Jackson, late captain of artillery, who had been directed by Gen. Polk to organize a cavalry regiment out of Logwood's Battalion and other companies of cavalry operating in that quarter   Only a temporary organization was effected at this place, Capt. Wm. H. Jackson being made colonel, and Maj. C. H. Hill, of Logwood's battalion, major.

While encamped here with the Twenty-first Tennessee Infantry, 616 strong, under Col. Ed Pickett, Jr., on garrison duty, the command was attacked at sunrise of March 31, by a force from Hickman, Ky., under Col. N. B. Buford, consisting of Twenty-seventh Illinois and Fifteenth Wisconsin Infantry, three companies of cavalry, and four guns, in all 1,350 men. The attack was a surprise, the commander being unaware of the enemy's approach until their pickets were driven in and cannon-balls plowing their camp. The regiment was unorganized and poorly armed, and the stampede was general, the infantry going over a high fence into a bottom, and the cavalry hunting the rear with celerity. If the enemy had pursued, the consequences would have been disastrous, as only a small force of infantry under Capts. Frazer and Persons and Lieut. Woltering remained, near the enemy under cover of the hill; while the cavalry, finding themselves unpursued, rallied to the rear and awaited the enemy's retreat with great patience. Not a gun was fired from our line during the affair; fourteen prisoners, mostly pickets and stragglers, were captured by the enemy. The garrison also lost twelve wagons and teams, and their encampment was burned by the enemy, who held possession of the town for two hours and then retired.

Company D (White's) of the regiment also lost their camp chests and records in the hurry of the retreat, and their company colors were left in a hut. Company B also lost their colors.

This little surprise rid the command, however, of the trunk nuisance, about fifty of these unsoldier-like pieces of luggage being captured by the enemy from the regiment. "I set in to be a soldier after that," remarked

Sergt. R. J Black, of Company B, whose trunk containing various books of poems and other luxuries was taken by the remorseless Federals. The surprise seems to have grown out of a contest between the two colonels present over the question of priority of rank.

This beginning was most inauspicious, but their ill fortune was soon to be redeemed by the newly fledged regiments. ("Rebel. Records," 8, p. 116.) After the Federals retreated the regiment was marched to Trenton, Tenn., thirty miles, in a furious rainstorm, and remained there several days without baggage in a muddy camp—a most valuable lesson. There they were thoroughly organized and fitted for service, taking the name of the First Tennessee Cavalry, by which title it was known for many months before its number, Seventh Tennessee Cavalry, was finally assigned. But in this narrative it will be known only as the Seventh Tennessee. On April 1, Gen. Beauregard sent an officer of his staff to investigate the surprise of Col. Pickett's command at Union City, and censured strongly, in a letter to Gen. Polk, the colonel for permitting it. ("Reb. Rec.," 10, pt. 2, p. 378.) April 5 to 10 the regiment was engaged in a scout toward Hickman.

Dresden, and Union City The colonel (Jackson) commanding, on his return, expressed great annoyance from the "Independent Companies" in his command, and urged their organization into one command (except Capt. Dillard's company) for the war or discharge from the service as expensive and useless camp followers. Haywood's company, afterward D, had not joined the regiment on the 10th of April, but came in and became a part of the regiment about April 15, 1862. ("Reb. Rec.," p. 407.)

April 29 the regiment was ordered by Gen. Beauregard to accompany Col. Thomas H. Claiborne in an expedition to Paducah for the purpose of capturing and destroying the immense army stores at that point, valued at $3,000,000.

On May 4 the expedition set out from McKenzie, consisting of Claiborne's Sixth Confederate Cavalry and the Seventh Tennessee, in all 1,250 men. They reached Paris in the afternoon, and learning there that the enemy's forces in that quarter had gone toward Dresden, marched on in the night, which was dark and rainy, in pursuit. Learning after midnight that their contemplated descent upon Paducah was known to the enemy, the commander in the morning determined to abandon the expedition to that city and to attack and destroy the force in their front under Maj. Schaefer, consisting of three companies of the Fifth Iowa Cavalry.

Overtaking them on the 5th, about 5 P.M., at Lockridge Mill, on the south fork of the Obion River, an attack was at once made by five companies under acting field officer Capt. Ballentyne. Coming first on the pickets, these were driven back on the main force, which was at once charged near and over the bridge and stampeded—the men rushing headlong among the enemy, who when overtaken generally fought gallantly. The pursuit was kept up for several miles, during which time the enemy's battalion was almost annihilated, their loss being six killed and sixteen wounded, including Maj. Schaefer mortally and Capts. Hass and Minden and Lieut. Smith slightly, and four officers and sixty-seven privates and non-commissioned officers captured, out of a total of one hundred and thirty. Capt. Ballentyne, of Company C, was greatly distinguished for his headlong gallantry in this charge, he engaging in several hand to hand combats, in all of which he was victor. Col. Claiborne describes the affair thus: "Capt. Ballentyne, of Col. Jackson's Cavalry, was acting field officer with five companies at the head of the column. His first company (B, Seventh Tennessee) was deployed as mounted skirmishers, and dashed on the pickets. The pickets were astonished, and let us approach to within seventy yards, then fired and turned to flee. A yell, a charge blown, a picket killed, and the five companies, followed by the whole command, swept the two miles away in seven minutes or less over the enemy, who had been in vain urged, as claimed afterward by their major, to rally, etc. The good conduct of Col. Jackson was as usual with him, such as to merit your highest approval, and the good conduct of his regiment on the march and in the affair excellent."

Of the enemy, Private Hoffman showed exceptional gallantry, fighting Capt. Ballentyne desperately with his saber and piercing his coat several times, but was finally slain. The command captured two wagons and fifty-six horses and many arms and accouterments, and all without the loss of a man. Sergt. Black, of Company B, was slightly wounded in the hand by a saber cut. In the onset Private L. J O'Kelly, of Company B, rushed to the front, and having discharged his gun and pistol, drew saber, and, overtaking one of the enemy's troopers, engaged him in personal combat. The fight was short, Private O'Kelly receiving a cut on the head, when the Federal trooper fled. His hurts were not ascertained. Private O'Kelly, however, remained in the combat, and soon after captured the enemy's quartermaster and brought him to head-quarters. And thus was the stain of the Union City surprise obliterated from its standard by the regiment.

On May 12 the regiment was ordered by Gen. Beauregard to guard the line from Brownsville to Forked Deer River by Ripley, and report to Gen. Villepigue at Fort Pillow

On May 15 Company D, Capt. J S White, was disbanded at Jackson, Tenn., the term of enlistment, twelve months, having expired. Most of the members re-enlisted in Companies A and B. Company K, Capt. S. F Taylor, joined the regiment here. May 24, 1862, the regiment was reorganized further as Confederate troops and sworn in for the war.

June 3 the regiment was ordered to cover the evacuation of Fort Pillow and the retreat of Gen. Villepigne's command. This safely accomplished, the regiment moved by easy marches by way of Brownsville, Durhamville, Ripley, Covington, Shelby Depot, Collierville, to Coldwater, Holly Springs, Miss., Lumpkin's Mills, and thence to Abbeville, on the Tallahatchie River, where they were joined by Companies L and M. Here, on June 10, 1862, the regiment was completely reorganized by order of Brig. Gen. Villepigue, electing a full complement of field officers, as shown in the following roster, to wit:

Colonel, W H. Jackson;
Lieutenant-colonel, J G Stocks;
Major, W L. Duckworth;
Surgeon, J T Marable;
Assistant Surgeon, J C. Ward;
Chaplain, B. F Crouch;
Assistant Commissary Subsistence, A. P Slover;
Assistant Quartermaster, W P Paul;
Adjutant, John W Somervell.

The company officers at this time were:

COMPANY A.

Captain, W F Taylor;
First Lieutenant, J W Snead;

Second Lieutenant. H. W Watkins;
Brevet Second Lieutenant, W L. Certain;
First Sergeant, J D. Mitchell;
Second Sergeant. H. P Woodard.
Third Sergeant, G A. Stovall;
Fourth Sergeant. W G. Richardson.
Fifth Sergeant, John F Graham;
First Corporal, H. F King;
Second Corporal, W H. Rollins;
Third Corporal, A. J Ivy;
Fourth Corporal, J. W Fairburn;
Bugler, H. L. Farmer;
Blacksmith, J O'Meara.

COMPANY B.

Captain, J P Russell;
First Lieutenant, H. T. Sale;
Second Lieutenant, P T Winn;
Brevet Second Lieutenant, I. N Stinson;
First Sergeant, R. J Black;
Second Sergeant. James A. Wardlow;
Third Sergeant, James R. Somerville;
Fourth Sergeant, R. H. Harper;
Fifth Sergeant. M. W Hilliard;
First Corporal, L. A. Burkhart;
Second Corporal, J P Pullen;
Third Corporal, T F Archer;
Fourth Corporal, R. P Archer;

Company C.

Captain, S. P Bassett;
First Lieutenant, John T. Lawler;
Second Lieutenant, W B. Winston;
Brevet Second Lieutenant, L. B. Higgins;
First Sergeant, John D. Huhn;
Second Sergeant, A. Hicks;
Third Sergeant, W D. Nicholson;
Fourth Sergeant, T. J Lewellyn;
Fifth Sergeant, James Abernathy;
First Corporal, Thomas Brocchns.

Company D.

Captain, L. W Taliaferro;
First Lieutenant, H. J Livingston;
Second Lieutenant, C. H. Read;
Brevet Second Lieutenant, T. B. Mann;
First Sergeant, J Eader;
Second Sergeant, W J Winfield;
Third Sergeant, M. McGrath;
Fourth Sergeant, J C. Holloway;
Fifth Sergeant, R. M. Grizzard;
First Corporal, J L. Elwood;
Second Corporal, E. D. Dupree;
Third Corporal, R. S. Irvine;
Fourth Corporal, D. Dodge.

COMPANY E.

Captain, W J Tate;
First Lieutenant, J P. Statler;
Second Lieutenant, H. Harris;
Brevet Second Lieutenant, W C. Mashburn;
First Sergeant, J W Nelson;
Second Sergeant, A. M Statler;
Third Sergeant, R. D. Durrett;
Fourth Sergeant, F Fentress;
Fifth Sergeant, W C. Hardy;
First Corporal, V F Ruffin;
Second Corporal, J V Field;
Third Corporal, Hardy Mashburn;
Fourth Corporal, C B. Linthicum.

COMPANY F

Captain, C C. Clay;
First Lieutenant, C H. Jones;
Second Lieutenant, J E. Gregory;
First Sergeant, W T Robinson;
Second Sergeant, J A. Everett;
Third Sergeant, G. W Richards;
Fourth Sergeant, James Sinclair;
Fifth Sergeant, J M. Baker.

COMPANY G

Captain, F F Aden;
First Lieutenant, J J Blake;

Second Lieutenant, J T Haynes;
First Sergeant, W A. Wright;
Second Sergeant, P J Diggs;
Third Sergeant, F F Diggs;
Fourth Sergeant, H. A. Humphreys;
First Corporal, L. P Atkinson;
Second Corporal, J R. Anderson;
Third Corporal, E. T Looney;
Fourth Corporal, J P Martin;

COMPANY H.

Captain, H. C McCutchen,
First Lieutenant, J A. Jenkins;
First Sergeant, W E. Martin;
Second Sergeant, J A. J Nowlin;
Third Sergeant, T J Franklin;
Fourth Sergeant, A. H. Johnson;
First Corporal, J W Mook;
Second Corporal, J M Goolsby;
Third Corporal, W J Barger;
Fourth Corporal, R. A. Rasa.

COMPANY I

Captain, J R. Alexander;
First Lieutenant, W P Malone;
Second Lieutenant, P. A. Fisher;
Brevet Second Lieutenant, E. M. Downing;
First Sergeant, John W Shelton;

Second Sergeant. H. P Colton;
Third Sergeant, John C Pace;
Fourth Sergeant, John H. Smith;
First Corporal, G W Orvall;
Second Corporal, James Ashton;
Third Corporal, A. M. Walk;
Fourth Corporal, James M. Barrett.

Company K.

Captain. Samuel F Taylor;
First Lieutenant. William F Broadnax;
Second Lieutenant, J I. Mullins;
Brevet Second Lieutenant, W E. Burleson;
First Sergeant, H. H. Elean;
Second Sergeant, J R. Coffield;
Third Sergeant, William Delaschmit;
Fourth Sergeant, L. F Taylor;
First Corporal, W J Westmoreland,
Second Corporal. R. Stephens;
Third Corporal, J L. Adkins;
Fourth Corporal, T H. Hutton.

Company L.

Captain. Alexander Duckworth;
First Lieutenant. Charles L. Taliaferro;
Second Lieutenant, Frank Pugh;
Brevet Second Lieutenant, William Witherspoon;

First Sergeant, R. D. Grove;
Second Sergeant, Thomas Nelson;
Third Sergeant, Thomas E. Rooks;
Fourth Sergeant, John V Baugh;
Fifth Sergeant, J C W Cobb;
First Corporal, M. H. Dupree;
Second Corporal, W L. Barnes.

Company M.

Captain, B. T Davis;
First Lieutenant, W H. Moorer;
Second Lieutenant, C S. O. Rice;
Brevet Second Lieutenant, J L. Livingston;
First Sergeant, J H. Mann;
Second Sergeant, J F Green;
Third Sergeant, H. W Keeler;
Fourth Sergeant, John Haywood;
First Corporal, T C Anthony;
Second Corporal, T A Walker;
Third Corporal, J D. Greavis;
Fourth Corporal, L. Moore.

Abbeville was thus, it seems, the birthplace of the regiment, which was still for some time known as the "First Tennessee," and its fighting career may be said to have been inaugurated here. From this period until the close of the war it, under successive commanders, preserved its orderly, compact organization, hardening rapidly into a regiment of veterans, whose fortitude, daring, and discipline through the succeeding bloody years of strife afford one of the brightest pages of the record of Confederate martial history

CHAPTER II.

Soldiers in Earnest—Capturing a Guarded Train—Severe Fighting at Bolivar, Medon, and Britton's Lane—A Reverse at Coldwater—The Charge at Davis's Bridge—Battle of Corinth—The Shooting of Captain Hill—A Stampede at Old Lamar—Covering the Retreat—The Fight at Coffeeville—Capture of Holly Springs—Companies B and A detached—Death of Chaplain Crouch—The Affair at Hernando—Attack on Collierville—Escape of Gen. Sherman.

In June, 1862, Col. Jackson, having completed the details of the regimental organization, and perfected the regiment somewhat in the drill, company and battalion, decided to test their soldiership by a rapid descent upon the enemy's lines of communication near La Fayette Station, Tenn. Moving from Byhalia June 24, 1862, and approaching the Memphis and Charleston railroad at this point June 25, a detachment was made of two squadrons of about twenty men each under Capts. Lawler and Tate, of Companies C and E, to reconnoiter the railroad, both east and west of La Fayette, and develop the position of the enemy's guards.

Capt. Lawler's party, finding no enemy in sight, displaced a rail in a curve and then formed near by under cover to await events. Pretty soon a train appeared and fell into the trap. But it was loaded with a detachment of Federal infantry of the Fifty-sixth Ohio Regiment under Col. Kinney, who at first were thrown into great confusion by this rude disembarkation and the fire of the little party from their cover, and fled incontinently toward La Fayette. But a short distance away they were rallied, and observing the paucity of the command which had given them such a fright, at once assumed the offensive. Capt. Lawler had in the meantime notified Col. Jackson of his "find," and that officer, bringing the regiment rapidly up on the flank of the enemy, by a vigorous attack stampeded their forces, capturing the train and fifty-six prisoners, including Col. Peter Kinney, their commander. A few of the train guards escaped to Germantown. This success and that at Lockridge's Mill gave the regiment a self-confidence and spirit which it retained throughout the war. ("Reb. Rec.," 17, pt. 1, p. 12.)

A letter in the *Memphis Appeal* of July 7, 1862, from the regiment, places the number of prisoners at 73, including Col. Peter Kinney, of Fifty-sixth Ohio, Lieut. Wellspaugh, of Twenty-ninth Illinois, 2 sergeants, 3 corporals, and 66 privates of the Twentieth Illinois, Fifty-sixth Ohio, Third, Second, and Eleventh Iowa, Tenth Missouri, and Twenty-sixth Illinois Regiments. The command fell back to Coldwater, and Col. Kinney was paroled on condition that he would secure the exchange of Col. Brown, of the Confederate service, captured at Island 10.

On the evening of June 30, 1862, a detachment of the regiment (number not given), under Maj. Duckworth, attacked a Federal wagon train and escort at Morning Sun, in Shelby County, Tenn. The train guard consisted of two hundred and forty men of the Fifty-seventh Ohio Infantry under Col. William Mungen, and the train contained sixty-seven wagons of the First Division, Army of Tennessee. The onset was sudden, and the train was in part stampeded, six of the wagons being wrecked. The detachment captured thirty-one mules with harness. Neither commander gives his own losses, but each estimates the loss of his antagonist as follows: Maj. Duckworth places the Federal loss at six killed and eight captured, and the

Federal commander charges Duckworth's loss to be nine killed and eighteen wounded. Gen. Grant, in a dispatch relating to the affair, admits a loss of three wounded and nine missing. These little affairs formed the subject of a complimentary notice (Gen. Order No. 93) by Gen. Bragg, commanding department at Tupelo. July 5, 1862.

GENERAL ORDER No. 93.

HEAD-QUARTERS DEPT. No. 2.
TUPELO, July 5, 1862.

The commander of the forces has to announce to the army a well-planned and soldierly executed expedition within the enemy's lines, led by Col. William H. Jackson, First Tennessee Cavalry, with a portion of his regiment, resulting in the capture of a Federal colonel and some fifty-six non-commissioned officers and privates, and the destruction of a locomotive and train of cars near La Fayette Station, Memphis and Charleston railroad, on the 25th ultimo.

On the 30 ultimo another detachment under the command of Maj. Duckworth, in the same vicinity, dashed upon the enemy's pickets and killed six and captured eight, with slight casualty to his command. These affairs are happy presages to the spirit with which this army is prepared to enter upon the impending campaign in emulation of the heroic deeds of our brothers in arms and in blood in Virginia.

By command of Gen. Bragg:

THOMAS JORDAN, Chief of Staff

Another letter in the *Appeal* (published at Grenada) of July 4, 1862, asserts that this attack at Morning Sun, on June 30, was made by Faulkner's and Porter's companies of partisans.

And Gen. Sherman also mentioned in a complimentary note the successful defense of the wagon train by Col. Mungen, which, he declared, "also inspired the men with more confidence when acting against the *dreaded cavalry*." ("Reb. Rec.," xvii., pt. 1, 10–12, 14–17.)

So it seems that under the cool soldiership of Col. Jackson the regiment was already dreaded by the powerful enemy.

After these affairs the regiment retired to Senatobia and encamped, and went thence to Hernando, Byhalia, and Abbeville.

On July 25 part of the regiment was assembled at Holly Springs under Col. Joseph Wheeler, who had superseded Gen. Chalmers, and started on a raid to West Tennessee, the entire party numbering about 1,000 men, about 500 of whom belonged to the Seventh Regiment.

The regiment marched to Grand Junction, which place was taken and some stores destroyed, but when about ten miles from Bolivar it was detached from the raiding party, and sent back southward by order of Gen. Villepigue, at Holly Springs. ("Reb. Rec.," xvii., pt. 1, p. 43.)

At the close of August, 1862, Col. Jackson was ordered by Gen. Van Dorn to accompany Gen. F C Armstrong, commanding a brigade composed of the Second Missouri, Second Arkansas, Second Tennessee, and Wirt Adams's Mississippi Cavalry, in all 1,600 men, in a raid on the enemy's communication along the line of the Mississippi Central railroad. Joining Gen. Armstrong at Holly Springs, Col. Jackson with his brigade (Seventh Tennessee and First Mississippi), 1,100 strong, moved rapidly by way of Grand Junction to Bolivar, in the vicinity of which place and five miles from Bolivar, on the Van Buren road, the command encountered the enemy on the morning of August 30, and a sharp fight ensued. The enemy, under Col. M. D. Leggett, consisted of the Twentieth and Seventy-eighth Ohio Infantry, four companies of the Second Illinois, and two companies of the Eleventh Illinois Cavalry, and a section of artillery (two guns) of the Ninth Indiana Battery The Confederate command was 2,600 strong, less detachments, and was composed of Armstrong's Brigade, 1,600 men,

and Jackson's Brigade of 1,100 men. The
fighting began early in the morning. Col.
Jackson's command advanced in front of
Gen. Armstrong's Division on the Van Buren road. The enemy opened at long range,
killing some horses. The van-guard pushed
rapidly forward, and soon after Gen. Armstrong moved with the greater part of his
command over to the Middleburg road, on
which the enemy seemed to be concentrating,
leaving Col. Jackson to guard the Van Buren
road, and watch the enemy in that quarter
Col. McCulloch, of the Second Missouri, led
a fierce charge on the enemy in front of Middleburg, driving them back, and killing
Lieut.-Col. Hogg, of the Second Illinois, but
lost the famous Capt. J R. Champion in the
charge Pressing up with both commands
from all sides, the enemy yielded, and fell
back rapidly to Bolivar. The enemy lost 5
killed, 18 wounded, and 71 prisoners. Bolivar being strongly fortified and garrisoned,
the command moved around it, and next day
attacked the detachments guarding the railroad between Bolivar and Medon, skirmished
at Toone's Station, destroyed the bridge and
one mile of trestle, and captured 40 prisoners. Appearing in front of Medon, the place

was found to be fortified and barricaded with cotton-bales, and guarded by four companies of the Forty-sixth Illinois Infantry, which were at once re-enforced by six companies of the Seventh Missouri Infantry

The place being too strong for capture, the command, after some fighting and considerable loss to the Seventh Tennessee, moved toward Denmark, and on next day, September 1, about 10 A.M., encountered Col. Dennis's command at Britton's Lane, the juncture of the Denmark and Medon roads.

Col. Dennis's command consisted of the Twentieth and Thirtieth Illinois Infantry Regiments, two companies of cavalry, and two pieces of artillery The fight was of the most desperate character, the enemy having the advantage of a chosen position in a grove on a ridge, surrounded by open corn-fields, and backed by broken grounds. The regiment made a furious charge mounted, getting within thirty feet of the enemy's lines. James Dillihunty, of Company B, among others, was killed in this charge After four hours' fighting, both sides tacitly agreed to quit. The Confederates captured the enemy's wagon train, a portion of which was destroyed, two pieces of artillery, and two hundred and thirteen prisoners. The enemy lost five killed and fifty-five wounded, but recaptured their artillery ("Reb. Rec.," xvii., 1, p. 50, etc.)

As above stated, the Confederate losses are not given in their engagements separately, but aggregated 115 all told during the entire raid.

The command recrossed the Hatchie River on the morning of September 2, and moved southward to Somerville on the next day, unpursued. In this series of engagements the command was in the saddle for more than forty-eight consecutive hours, mostly without food, and fought three pitched battles with as many different commands of the enemy, and came away unmolested with their captured property and prisoners. The latter were paroled after crossing Hatchie River on September 2.

The commands then separated; Gen. Armstrong's Brigade joining Gen. Price in Eastern Mississippi, and Col. Jackson's Brigade rejoining Gen. Van Dorn in North Mississippi near Holly Springs. On September 8, 1862, Col. Jackson sent a detachment of four companies, including Company A, Seventh Tennessee, and three companies of the First Mississippi under Lieut.-Col. Montgomery, toward Hernando. Returning on Tuesday the 9th, they met the Federals near Byhalia, 370 strong, under Col. Grierson. Lieut.-Col. Montgomery's advance guards were not well out, and the Federals charged his battalion while he was trying to form them, and drove them back in some disorder across the bridge over Coldwater, which they burned. Our loss was two killed and five wounded, including Private Tom Harris, killed with saber, and Privates Rod Clarkson, W J. Bynum, and R. E. Cayce, of Company A, severely, and Private Wilburn, of the same company, mortally wounded. After the Federals retreated, Lieut.-Col. Montgomery, who had rallied his men, re-occupied the ground. The Federal loss was reported as one killed and four wounded and seven horses. After rejoining Gen. Van Dorn, the regiment moved with that commander northward, being again in the vicinity of Bolivar on September 20, and returning thence south-eastward at sundown on the 25th, surprised and almost annihilated a force of 290 of the enemy's cavalry at Davis's Bridge, eight miles west of Chewalla. The enemy consisted of 200 of the Eleventh Illinois and 90 men of the Fifteenth Michigan, all under Lieut.-Col. McDermott, of the last-named regiment. Pinson led the charge at the bridge and into their camp, being seriously wounded in the onset. The Seventh Tennessee, under Lieut.-Col. Stocks, followed into the midst of the fight, and the rout was complete. The enemy for the most part were in a field cutting corn when the attack was made, and scattered and got away the best they could. The enemy lost 140 men killed, wounded, and captured, including 63 prisoners. The loss of the Seventh was nothing at all. ("Reb. Rec.," 17, pt. 1, p. 143, 144.)

This was one of the most brilliant affairs of the year. The regiment was then marched to Ripley, where, on the 27th of September, Price and Van Dorn effected a junction and moved north-eastwardly to attack Corinth. On the first of October the regiment was at Pocahontas, and turning sharply eastward was again at Davis's Bridge on the same day, and on the 2d of October drove in the enemy's pickets at Chewalla, losing Private John Young, of Company A, killed, and encamped in front of the enemy that night, a few miles from Corinth. Next day, October 3, the regiment marched to Corinth, and the battle began.

Companies G and H were detached and acted as an advance guard to Gen. Price's

Division, and the remainder of the brigade moved *en echelon* on Gen. Lovell's right, south of the Memphis and Charleston railroad. Night stopped the combat, and on the next day the brigade again moved forward in line, its left resting on the Memphis and Charleston railroad. Col. Jackson, with eight companies, during this day's battle made a *reconnaissance* to the southward of Corinth, driving off a force of the enemy's cavalry in that quarter

Later in the day the brigade was advanced to the fortifications on College Hill, where it maintained a hot combat after the army had withdrawn, after which it slowly withdrew and covered the rear of the retreating army Companies G and H, still with Gen. Price, built the bridge over the Hatchie at Crum's Mills, across which the defeated army effected its escape from the converging armies of Ord and Rosecrans, in the direction of Davis's Bridge. On the 5th these two companies, marching in the rear of Gen. Bowen's Brigade, confronted and vigorously repulsed, with the Mississippi battalion, a charge in force of the enemy's cavalry on the rear of that brigade, which was the extreme rear guard of the army (Bowen's report. "Reb. Rec.," 17, pt. 1, p. 413.)

The regiment was now ordered to Rienzi, and marched to Kossuth, returning thence to the vicinity of Pocahontas, one and a half miles from which place on the Ripley road it engaged the enemy in a hot skirmish, thereby aiding to save the army trains which had been parked between the Tuscumbia and Hatchie Rivers. Bivouacking here that night, on next day the brigade covered the rear of the army, fighting all the way to Ripley The last three days of this movement the regiment was without rations, and had to subsist the best they could on the country The colonel commanding, in his report, complimented specially Lieut. H. W Watkins, of Company A, and Corporal Brocchus and Privates Britton and Barton, of Company C, for gallantry and efficiency in the field. (Jackson's report. "Reb. Rec.," 17, pt. 1, p. 384.)

On September 30, 1862, occurred one of those instances of brutality which were rarely seen in either army, to their honor be it said, but were too frequently exhibited in certain Federal commands in West Tennessee and North Mississippi in 1862–63, and which were the legitimate outgrowth of the unconcealed sentiment of a few Federal officers of high rank in those districts, whose expressed opinion was that the war should be made one of extermination. Happily, better counsels or a stronger will prevailed, and so was averted a state of war that. pushed to its conclusion as desired by those inhuman officers, would have horrified the earth by scenes of blood unequaled in modern warfare. It would have converted the splendid and brave Federal army into a horde of butchers and made of every Southern man and boy a wild beast of prey. lying in wait for their enemy and slaying him pitilessly whenever found. Whether we are indebted for escape from this unnatural state of warfare to the soldierly manliness of Grant or the kindly heart of Lincoln, history has not yet disclosed. The incident referred to, and which is only narrated here because relating to the Seventh Tennessee regimental history, was the capture and shooting of Capt. Lafayette Hill, of Company I, and is thus described by the Federal commander, Col. F. A. Starling, of the Seventy-second Illinois, in whose command it occurred.

"I have also to mention an unfortunate occurrence where the man Rose was arrested as reported to me by Capt. De Golyer. A Capt. Hill, of Jackson's rebel cavalry, was at the place on sick leave. He at first attempted to escape. Finding it impossible, he surrendered himself to Capt. De Golver, and while talking with him, one of Capt. Moore's men. Private Gottlieb Lippold, came up in an excited manner, and said to Capt. Hill, 'Point your pistol at me, damn you,' and fired; the ball entering the thigh, making a serious flesh wound. Capt. Moore, when he came up, said his man had done right: 'He ought to have shot him through the head.' I reprimanded Capt. Moore. He seemed to think his man was right. I mention the fact that the matter, if necessary, can be thoroughly investigated." (Col. F. A. Starling's report, "Reb. Rec.," 17, pt. 1. p. 148.)

No action was taken to avenge this treatment of one of its officers by the Seventh Regiment.

On November 8, 1862, the advance of the enemy under Gen. McPherson was encountered by the First Mississippi Brigade and Seventh Tennessee under Lieut.-Col. Montgomery at Old Lamar, Miss., about seven miles south of La Grange. The enemy's force consisted of two divisions of infantry and 1,200 calvary (Seventh Kansas, Second Illinois, and Third Michigan), the latter under

Col. A. L. Lee. The enemy attacked with Johnson's Brigade of Infantry, and while Jackson's Brigade was stoutly resisting this attack, with their left flank well guarded, the enemy's cavalry discovered an unguarded point on the right, and threw their cavalry around to our rear Discovering their presence, the command retreated, but not knowing the exact position of the enemy, ran into them, and supposing themselves surrounded, were thrown into great confusion. The flight and panic was general, and not at all creditable, the men falling over some wounded horses in the road, and into the deep ditches pell-mell.

The following members of the regiment were captured, all wounded or bruised from falling over the dead horses and into the ditches in the stampede: L. W Taliaferro, Company D; C. C. Clay, Company F; L. B. Claiborne, Company D; J. A. Ross, Company H; Second Lieut. J A. Jenkins, Company H; J M. Meek, Company H; First Lieut. W R. Jones, Company H; J W Flanagan, Company I; N. J Franckthem, Company I; J A. Yarboro, Company I; J D. Smith, Company I; R. L. Smith, Company I; Nat Williams, Company I; Second Lieut. J R. Alexander, Company I; G W Walton, Company I; C J Fisher, Company I; J. P Overall, Company I; also Lieut. I. N Stinson and Privates W H. Strange and John Smith, of Company B; also Lieut. W B. Winston, of Company C, who gave the correspondent, "Mack," of the *Cincinnati Commercial*, some tart opinions about the emancipation proclamation and other matters relating to the Federal conduct of the war.

Private L. B. Claiborne, one of the wounded of Company D, died in the Federal hospital at La Grange on November 11, 1862, attended by his faithful colored boy, who was captured with him. A number of the First Mississippi Cavalry were wounded and captured at the same place. The captured men were at once paroled and started to Vicksburg for exchange.

The regiment was encamped now for awhile at Chulahoma, and skirmished near Holly Springs November 12, 1862.

On November 22 the regiment was encamped ten miles south of Holly Springs and engaged in outpost duty, the advance of Grant's immense army of invasion being at that time between La Grange and Davis's Mills. The weather was very cold.

November 28, 1862, the enemy advanced,

driving the pickets out of Holly Springs, and on the 29th attacked Jackson at Waterford. where he fought them with part of his command and two guns. On the 29th and 30th the regiment fell back slowly, fighting at intervals; part of the regiment, including Company B, having a skirmish at Chulahoma on the 30th, retreated thence by way of Toby Tubby ferry, and Sunday night marched through torrents of rain to Oxford. Griffith's and McCulloch's Brigades had been detached, and only Jackson's old brigade, First Mississippi and Seventh Tennessee, remained at the front on this road. Tuesday, December 2, in the morning, the regiment moved out seven miles north of Oxford and had a sharp fight, and retiring, the enemy appeared and attacked the outposts in front of Oxford. Adjutant Joe Wicks, of the Seventh, was killed while engaged with Col. Ballentyne about noon north of town on the Wyatt road. When the Federals entered the town, about 4:30 o'clock in the afternoon, Col. Jackson endeavored to lead to the charge a regiment of infantry which were formed in the public square; but the men, being drunk, would not follow By night the command had all left Oxford, and the cavalry under Jackson picketed the hills to the south, and next day, December 3, crossed Yocona River.

A powerful force of the enemy, consisting of nine regiments of cavalry with artillery, under Col. T L. Dickey followed the retreating army, marching toward Water Valley and Coffeeville. On December 4 a heavy skirmish was had with this command at Springdale Bridge, which had attempted to cut off the retreat of the cavalry rear-guard, the enemy being repulsed. On December 5 the enemy appeared in front of Coffeeville with the brigades of Lee, Hatch, and Mizner, about four thousand strong, and were at once assailed by Gen. Tighlman's division of infantry, one thousand three hundred strong, supported by Col. Jackson's Seventh Regiment, seven hundred strong, under Capt. McCutchen, and though fighting gallantly, were driven back three miles. The fighting was very severe, the regiment losing several men. Among the wounded were Privates J B. Mills and John F McCallum, of Company A, the last named, a boy of fifteen years, being permanently disabled. The Confederate loss was 7 killed, 43 wounded, and 10 missing. The enemy's loss was 10 killed, 63 wounded, and 41 captured. The enemy retreated in haste to Oxford. Part of Company

K was consolidated with Company B at Coffeeville December 12, 1862. About the 15th of December Gen. Van Dorn concentrated about twenty-five hundred men, including the Seventh Tennessee, at Grenada, and moved north-eastward December 16 with great speed toward Pontotoc, reaching that place on the 18th, or as Gen. Grant expressed it, "Traveled as fast as the scouts who brought the news." Passing unawares by a large force in that quarter under Col. Dickey, who considered himself fortunate to escape unobserved, the command on the 20th, about sunrise, charged headlong into Holly Springs.

The enemy were taken completely by surprise. The town contained a garrison consisting of parts of the Twentieth and Sixty-second Illinois Infantry and the Second Illinois Cavalry and some sick in hospital, commanded by Col. R. C. Murphy, of the Eighth Wisconsin Infantry, in all nearly two thousand men, of which one thousand four hundred and forty-nine were captured, including their commander, Col. Murphy

The enemy, especially the cavalry, made some resistance, but were soon overcome and for the most part captured. The town contained vast army stores, amounting to $1,500,000, all of which was destroyed. This brilliant achievement of Gen. Van Dorn in moving around an army of 70,000 men, and through a cavalry force of double his numbers to the line of the enemy's communication in his rear at Holly Springs and capturing and destroying his depot of supplies, was one of the notable cavalry affairs of the war, and caused Gen. Grant to report to Gen. Halleck December 25, 1862 "It is perfectly impracticable to go farther South by this route, depending on the road for supplies, and the country does not afford them." ("Reb. Rec.," 17, pt. 1, p. 478.)

The result was an immediate retreat of the whole Federal army, January 8, from North Mississippi, and Corinth was in some measure redeemed. The regiment bore its full share in this movement, and won additional distinction for courage and devotion.

Next day, or December 21, the command attacked the intrenched position of the enemy at the crossing of Wolf River or Davis's Mills. The enemy, consisting of detachments of the Twenty-fifth Indiana and Fifth Ohio Regiments and one company of cavalry, had fortified the mill, converting it into a block-house by means of cross-ties and cotton-bales, and also erected strong earth-works, the two intrenchments covering and enfilading the bridge, from which the block-house was distant only seventy yards. The place was impregnable without artillery, of which the regiment had none; but the assault was made at 12 o'clock noon, with great vigor and dismounted. Twice the bridge was charged, and once a few of the men got across and found shelter under the structure; but the intrenchments were too strong to be taken, and the regiment lost considerably in their desperate attempts to effect their capture. The fighting was all done in an open field with an enemy entirely concealed and sheltered, and after about three hours' combat the regiment reluctantly withdrew, taking off sixteen prisoners whom they had captured in the vicinity The enemy's commander, Col. William H. Morgan, of the Twenty-fifth Indiana, recklessly claimed that the attacking force was a command six thousand strong, and that they left 22 dead, 30 wounded, and 20 prisoners in his hands, and left 30 men wounded in a house near by

Withdrawing from before this hornets' nest, the regiment went forward and was engaged in the combats of Bolivar on the 23d and 24th of December, which place, intrenched and defended by three regiments of infantry and three regiments of cavalry, was found to be too strong for capture, and the command withdrew A regiment of Texans under Col. Griffith attacked the block-house at Middleburg on the 24th, but were unsuccessful. Finding the enemy concentrating from every direction to affect its capture, the command withdrew by way of Ripley, New Albany, and Pontotoc to Grenada, followed to the vicinity of Pontotoc by the enemy in great force under Col. Grierson, with whom there was much unprofitable skirmishing about Ripley, with slight loss.

1863.

Early in the beginning of 1863 many changes took place in the structure of the regiment. Col. Jackson was promoted to brigadier-general, and assigned to a command under Van Dorn in Middle Tennessee, taking with him as an escort Company A, under Capt. W F Taylor Lieut.-Col. Stocks was made colonel, but soon resigned on account of ill health, and until fall the regiment had but a single field officer. Maj. W L. Duckworth became lieutenant-colonel. Company B was detailed for special service with Gen. Loring. After Company B was detached and ordered to report to Maj.-Gen. Loring at Canton for special duty, it was ordered to move to and go into camp on the Yazoo City road, where it performed outpost and courier duty for some time. It was then engaged in collecting laborers to work on the fortifications at Yazoo City, Fort Pemberton, and other places along the Yazoo River. They then rejoined Gen. Loring, and served on special duty with his army They were engaged in all the operations looking to the relief of Vicksburg, in the early summer of 1863, and in the siege of Jackson which followed, and the retreat from Jackson to Meridian, returning with Gen. Loring to Canton in the early winter, where they resumed quarters, doing special duty until February. 1864. when they were ordered to report back to the regiment at Grenada, and rejoined the regiment on February 8.

Company C, under Capt. Lawler, was sent to the vicinity of Memphis, to observe the movements of the enemy and protect Maj. Simmons, who was collecting supplies in that quarter, where they had concentrated an immense army preparatory to the descent upon Vicksburg. The remainder of the regiment was marched to Fort Pemberton, thence to

Greenwood, Miss., March 23, 1863, at the junction of the Tallahatchie and Yazoo Rivers, to operate in conjunction with the command of Gen. Loring, who was disputing the passage of Gen. Grant's army through the Yazoo Pass. Here, in the muddy bottoms and swamps of the Mississippi, they did much hard service, and suffered great exposure. January 24, 1863, E. H. Munford, of Company I, died of typhoid fever, near Charleston, Miss.; and in February. 1863, A. J. Foster died in the hospital at Grenada. On March 27 Private Robinson was accidently killed while turkey hunting.

In March the regiment was ordered back to Panola, in North Mississippi, and was, with Col. Slemmon's Second Arkansas and Col. McCulloch's First Missouri Regiments, constituted a Brigade of Cavalry, under Gen. James R. Chalmers, who was appointed Chief of Cavalry in North Mississippi. March 4 Company A was engaged in the series of conflicts at Franklin and Spring Hill, Tenn., which resulted in the capture, by Van Dorn's command, of Col. Coburn's large force of Federals, in that vicinity On March 31 Company A, together with one company, Armstrong's escort of the Twenty-eighth Mississippi, made one of those furious charges into the town of Franklin which were characteristic of the Confederate troopers in the West, losing several men—viz., Private Ed Starnes, killed, and Privates T W Armstrong, J. M. Riviere, Joe Kendrick, and J. L. Pruden, wounded.

This charge was so daring as to attract universal attention, and evoked from Gen. Jackson the following mention, viz.:

GENERAL ORDER NO. 10.

NEAR SPRING HILL, TENN., April 10, 1863.

High mention is due, also, to my escort, Capt. W H. [F.] Taylor commanding, for the fearless manner in which, on the 31st of March and to-day, they charged superior forces, with great success.

W H. JACKSON, *General Commanding.*

The last-named was a counter charge by the company on a charging battalion of Federals at Bird's house, near Thompson's Station.

On March 5, 1863, Chaplain Ben F Crouch, of the Seventh Regiment, was killed while fearlessly exposing himself on staff duty at Spring Hill. The story, in some way, got abroad that this accomplished minister and sturdy soldier, in the excitement of the battle, threw off his clerical dignity, and "swore like a trooper." It is pleasant to note that Gen.

W H. Jackson, in a letter to the *Memphis Appeal* (then published at Jackson, Miss.) of May 14, 1863, authoritatively denied this cruel slander, declaring that Rev Mr. Crouch was near him all day, and that no such thing occurred.

During April and May, 1863, the command was, under Gen. Chalmers, engaged in guarding the disputed frontier of North Mississippi, and observing the movements of the enemy, and skirmished with them near Senatobia, May 18, without loss In June, Gen. Chalmers marched with part of his command, four companies of Seventh Tennessee, four companies Second Arkansas, two companies of Faulkner's, and three guns, on an expedition to the Mississippi River about fifty miles below Memphis, where he was for some time engaged in shelling the river transports with some small smooth-bore guns. The enemy, learning of his contemplated movement, sent out a picked command from Memphis, consisting of 320 men from First Missouri, Second Illinois, and Fifth Ohio Regiments, under Maj. John Henry, to intercept him. This command was encountered by Gen. Chalmers June 19, 1863, about four miles south-west of Hernando, at Atkin's farm, and at once attacked, just after daylight. The

Seventh Regiment was drawn up on a hill and the enemy on another opposite, with a ravine or depression between. Firing rapidly, the regiment, under Col. Stocks, charged, mounted, down this hill and up the next, the immediate enemy—namely, the First Missouri—giving away and scampering to the rear in hot haste. The enemy's force, being assailed on all sides by Chalmers, was almost annihilated, the command taking eighty-eight prisoners, including the major and a lieutenant. The enemy's loss has been estimated as high as twenty or thirty killed and wounded. The Confederate loss was one killed and ten wounded, including Lieut. R. J Black, of Company B, shot through the thigh in the charge down the hill, and Adjt. W S. Pope and Capt. W J Tate, of Company E, wounded. The enemy were pursued fifteen miles on the road toward Memphis, and seemed to throw away nearly all the guns they had, so profuse was the quantity scattered on the field and by the way-side.

During the contest Capt. Lawler, with Company C, was marching rapidly to overtake the regiment, and unexpectedly encountered Gen. Wisener's Federal command of more than 1,000 men, which was just preparing to pounce upon the wagon train of Gen. Chalmers, near the

Coldwater River. Dispatching notice to the commander of the wagon train as to his peril, Capt. Lawler placed his company in ambush at Matthews's Ferry over the Coldwater, and awaited the enemy. They came winding down the high, steep bluff, unaware of danger, and intent on their prey, the wagon train. When the company opened fire there was an immediate stampede back over the bluff by the enemy, who suffered considerable loss. Then followed elaborate preparations by the powerful enemy for crossing the stream, which delayed them for several hours. Moving then across the stream, they were confronted by the little company, numbering less than thirty men, in open skirmish order, who took every advantage afforded by the timber and morasses in the bottom for obstructing the enemy's advance, to such an extent that the train, by tremendous exertion, was enabled to effect its escape to the main body of the command. After their return from this expedition, which was without further result, the regiment was engaged the remainder of the summer in drilling and scouting to various places in North Mississippi and West Tennessee. Early in October Gen. Chalmers led his brigade on an expedition to the enemy's lines at Collierville, Tenn.

October 5 the regiment moved into and occupied Holly Springs. It was commanded on this and the succeeding operations by Lieut.-Col. Duckworth up to the affair at Collierville. (See his report of October 20, 1862; also Chalmers's report of same date.)

It was then ordered to Coldwater, and to assault the enemy at Lockhart's Mills on October 6. While Company C skirmished with them, the Eighteenth Mississippi was ordered to cross above the mills and get in the enemy's rear, while the Seventh Tennessee and Third Mississippi, with the artillery, assaulted in front. But the artillery commander was too eager, and fired off one of his guns prematurely, which caused a premature attack by the Eighteenth Mississippi; and the enemy, though in large force, escaped before the regiment got in range.

The enemy was encountered October 8 at Salem, and a hot fight ensued. The Seventh Regiment was in reserve in the rear of the Eighteenth Mississippi until late in the action, when it was ordered to support the Second Missouri and Eighteenth Mississippi, which were being pressed back in the center. Arriving there and dismounting, the regiment charged vehemently on the enemy in front, driving them headlong from the field, and pursuing about two miles, until stopped by darkness. In this affair the command lost 1 killed and 27 wounded. Moving thence to Collierville on the morning of the 11th of October, the command surprised the enemy's post at that point about 9 o'clock A.M. A train had just arrived from Memphis, bringing Gen. Sherman and staff, and was endeavoring to move off. But failing, that wily warrior, retiring quietly to the depot building with the force at his disposal, which altogether consisted of the Sixty-sixth Indiana, and detachments of the Sixth and Seventh Illinois Cavalry and Thirteenth United States Regular Infantry, barricaded it, and together with the strong fort a short distance to the northward, made a desperate resistance to the assault of the eager Confederates, until Gen. Corse's Division of Infantry, then on the march from Memphis, hearing the firing, came rapidly up and brought the combat to an end. Lieut.-Col. Duckworth here commanded a demi-brigade, composed of the Seventh Tennessee and Second Missouri. The Seventh was commanded by Capt. John T Lawler, and the Second Missouri by Lieut.-Col. McCulloch. Lieut.-Col. Duckworth, receiving orders to attack from the west, dispatched

Lieut.-Col. McCulloch with the small detachment of his regiment on hand to the north side of the railroad, while the Seventh Regiment moved on the enemy's rifle-pits between McCulloch's and Neely's Regiments. The charge being ordered, the two regiments moved forward in a run, and with loud cheers drove the enemy out of his rifle-pits and into the fort and depot, and took possession of the trains standing at the depot. Finding they could go no farther without assistance, Lieut.-Col. Duckworth ordered them back from under fire. But receiving orders to burn the train, the charge was again ordered, and the regiment sprung forward and recaptured the train and burned two cars, using the shirts of Gen. Sherman and his staff for kindling the fire. (Sherman's report.) The other cars could not be fired for want of combustibles. Having accomplished this object right under the walls of the depot, which had been loop-holed and fortified, the regiment withdrew, as it was evident the fort was too strong for capture. In the first charge, Capt. John T Lawler, in command of the regiment, was shot four times; when Capt. Alexander Duckworth, of Company L, took command. But he was quickly shot also, and the command of the regiment devolved on Lieut. H. J Livingston, of Company D, who greatly distinguished himself in leading the second charge and by his skillful handling of his new command on the subsequent retreat. Lieut.-Col. Duckworth also speaks in his report in the highest terms of praise of Lieuts. J. P Statler and P A. Fisher, of Companies E and I, "for conspicuous bravery, being always foremost in the charge and first to reach the post of danger."

The Confederates, being unaware that the famous Federal commander was concealed in the depot building, turned their artillery mainly upon the fort, thus enabling him to escape, as they could easily have blown the little depot into the air. The regiment was in the forefront of this terrific fight, and suffered considerable loss. The enemy's infantry, being perfectly sheltered behind strong works, used their long Springfield rifles with deadly effect. The brigade lost 3 killed and 48 wounded, the regiment losing 2 killed and 13 wounded. The command captured 135 prisoners in this combat. Gen. Chalmers was wounded in one of the charges. Col. Richardson taking command of the division.

The command being hotly pursued as it retired, the Seventh Regiment was placed in the rear, and under the skillful direction of Lieut. H. J Livingston, of Company D, the then senior officer left, made successful resistance to all the assaults of the enemy on the rear-guard all the way from Ingram's Mills to the Tallahatchie River at Wyatt, where the enemy were finally repulsed and retired. Neither Companies A. B, nor G were in this fight; the first being still on duty with Gen. Jackson in Central Mississippi; and the latter, under Capt. F F Aden, being in West Tennessee recruiting. Company B, during the time, was in West Tennessee with Gen. Tyree H. Bell recruiting. (MSS. notes of Capt. Aden.)

On November 3 the command was again in the vicinity of Collierville, Tenn., and had some hot skirmishing there, and on the next day, November 4, attacked the Federal force at Moscow under Col. Hatch. The fighting here was quite severe and attended with considerable loss on both sides. On the same day Companies C and D, under Capt. L. W Taliaferro, of the last-named company, being detached, assailed the Federal block-house at Grissom's Creek, near La Fayette Station, surprising the enemy completely, whom they found outside the works playing cards. That intrepid commander charged with his two companies, mounted, right into the midst of them, and springing from their horses, entered the block-house together with the garrison, and compelled the surrender of the whole Federal force, amounting to one company The enemy in this day's combat lost 3 killed, 4 wounded, and 41 missing.

About October 1, 1863, Capt. C. C Clay, of Company F, was made major, and Maj. Duckworth, having previously become lieutenant-colonel by seniority, on November 10, 1863, was commissioned colonel of the regiment.

The regiment, after the affair at Moscow, had but little to do until Forrest commenced his first raid into West Tennessee, on which occasion it was thrown forward, December 3, across the Tallahatchie to assist in giving a good start to the movement; and again on December 28, when it marched northward from Como to cover Gen. Forrest's return from the raid, meeting him somewhat north of that place and returning thence to camp, December 31, 1863, just in time to get shelter from the coldest weather that had been experienced within man's memory in that latitude. The men suffered terribly, however, before they finally found shelter from the piercing cold.

CHAPTER III.

Under Gen. Forrest—Assigned to the Fourth Brigade—Affair at Okolona—Battle of Prairie Mound—Death of Col. Forrest—Repulse of the Federal Onset—The March to West Tennessee—Capture of Union City—The Ruse of Col. Duckworth—Under Gen. Rucker—Battle of Tishomingo Creek—Lieut.-Col. Taylor's Charge—The Fight for Possession of the Thicket—Death of Adjt. Pope—Rout of the Enemy—The A. J. Smith Raid—Battle of Harrisburg—The Regiment's Charge on the Works—Frightful Slaughter of the Men—Rescuing the Flag—Death of Capt. Statler—The Pursuit—Lieut.-Col. Taylor Takes Command.

AFTER some preliminary preparations, Gen. Forrest issued General Order No. 1, at Como, Miss., constituting the new provisional organization of cavalry in Forrest's Cavalry Department, embracing West Tennessee and North Mississippi. By General Order No. 3 of same date the Seventh Tennessee was embraced in the Fourth Brigade, Col. Jeffrey E. Forrest, which, with the Second Brigade, Col. McCulloch, constituted Chalmers's Division. In the Fourth Brigade were McDonald's Battalion, Seventh Tennessee, and Third, Fifth, and Nineteenth Mississippi Regiments. About

CAPT JOHN T LAWLER

ADJT JOHN D HUHN

LIEUT COL W F TAYLOR

LIEUT H J BLACK

LIEUT W B WINSTON

this time the regiment was ordered with the brigade to Panola, Miss., and remained until February 7, when it was detached and ordered, together with McDonald's Battalion, to Grenada under Col. J E. Forrest to observe a movement of Federals up the Yazoo River. About the 13th of February Col. Forrest, with this force, was ordered to move rapidly eastward to West Point, and marched that day and night in a heavy rain-storm. Proceeding on this march, the command was overtaken about the 18th of February by Gen. Forrest in the vicinity of Starksville, Miss., and thrown through West Point and north-eastward toward Aberdeen, to get in advance and check a formidable movement of the enemy under Gens. W S. Smith and Grierson from Memphis and other points on the Memphis and Charleston railroad, whose objective point was the fertile prairie region, the vicinity of which they had now reached. Meeting the enemy February 19, between Aberdeen and Egypt Station, the regiment skirmished lightly as they were slowly pressed back toward West Point. At one point the enemy, while pressing up hotly in front, sent a large force on the flank to endeavor to get in the rear of the brigade. This movement was almost successful, and when discovered by the regiment they fell back rapidly, running the gantlet of a brigade formation of the enemy on the roadside. In this race. L. H. Poindexter, of Company B, had his horse shot and was captured by the enemy, singularly enough our only loss. The brigade, being overtaken by Gen. Forrest several miles north of West Point, was retired across the Sookatoncha Bridge, four miles west of West Point. Here the enemy were held in check until the next morning, when after severe fighting, about noon the enemy began to retire and was at once followed by Gen. Forrest with a force of two brigades, including the Seventh Tennessee. Four miles north of West Point they encountered the enemy formed in some post oak timber at the edge of the prairie in the mouth of a lane and across a narrow causeway and bridge. After sharp fighting at close quarters, the enemy were driven back to their main line in the woods.

The men, being now dismounted, attacked vigorously a force perhaps four times their numbers, and forced them back to a position behind a strong picket fence in the prairie a half-mile long. The men of the command were almost frenzied now because of the burning by the Federal forces of hundreds of dwelling-houses, and the turning of the helpless inhabitants out unsheltered into the cold, wintery air, and fought with a desperation rarely assumed by them at any other time in the war Besides, this was their first fighting under their new commander, Forrest, and his immediate presence seemed to inspire every one with his terrible energy, which was more like that of a piece of powerful steam machinery than of a human being. Being assailed in the rear by a regiment, the enemy gave way, and the brigade charging and gaining the fence, opened fire behind it hotly on the rear of the retreating enemy Remounting, the pursuit was now as vigorous as the prairie mud would permit, and the men were often in sharp collision with the Federal troopers, who fought with unwonted gallantry After night-fall the brigade bivouacked in the abandoned camp of the enemy, where they found much forage and subsistence, and the camp-fires were especially grateful.

Reveille at 4 o'clock A.M. on the 22d, and before dawn the regiment, under Col. Duckworth, was in the saddle and pressing the pursuit toward Okolona, now fourteen miles ahead. The brigade was ordered by Gen. Forrest to take a left-hand road about nine miles from Okolona so as to reach the Pontotoc road in the rear of the Federals and intercept their retreat in that direction. Unable from the heavy road and the rapid retreat of the enemy to get in their rear, the brigade came upon them five miles from Okolona, strongly posted upon a high ridge covered with scrub oak and brushwood. The whole command, Bell's, Jeffrey Forrest's, and McCulloch's Brigades, were assembled here in the presence of the enemy, and Forrest's Brigade was ordered to attack to the right of the road. The attack was made with great fury, and the first line was quickly carried in the brigade's front, but in storming the second line, a short distance rearward, the fire encountered was terrible, and the men were cut down in great numbers, Col. Jeffrey Forrest, their commander, being among the slain. He was shot through the neck while charging, mounted, at the head of his men in a lane within fifty yards of the Federal works. Col. Duckworth, of the Seventh Tennessee, then took command of the brigade, Maj. Clay assuming the command of the regiment. The men sprung forward again, and the enemy were forced back, fighting gallantly, to a new position, under cover of rail piles and breastworks.

Being dismounted, the regiment was now led by Gen. Forrest in person, who called for the old Seventh, and after hard fighting the Federals were forced back again another half a mile. Col. Barksdale, of the Fifth Mississippi, was slain in this charge. The enemy again confronting, their line under cover and in strong force, the brigade marched forward and again carried the line in their front, but with serious loss in killed and wounded. About a mile further, at a group of log cabins, the enemy again made a stand. The Second and Seventh Tennessee here led the charge on the right under Gen. Forrest in person, with McCulloch's men on the left. The fire was deadly and for awhile seemed almost unbearable. Charging through the garden of one of the houses, Gen. Forrest's horse was shot, but alighting on his feet, he seized the gun of a fallen private and shouted to the men: "Forward!" At this point Maj. C. C. Clay, of the Seventh, was shot, the ball furrowing the top of his cranium, and Sergt. A. L. Elean, of Company B, was wounded by his side. Capt. Aden took command of the regiment, and the line marched forward steadily, driving the enemy back to a ridge on the west side of an open field, but the gallant Col. McCulloch was wounded and disabled in the charge. Here the enemy's cavalry, in four heavy lines, charged in turn upon the eager but disorganized men who had charged into the field, and now hastily drew back behind a willow slough, and the last and most determined of the brave troopers, supposed to have been the Fourth United States Regulars, broke through the Confederate alignment in several places, but meeting Col. McCulloch's men in the rear, were driven back with great loss. In these charges the men threw down their useless, empty guns, and drawing their revolvers, fought their assailants with the greatest fury at muzzle quarters. The regiment, though its line was thus broken, by no means gave way an inch, but held their position with undying courage.

Gen. Forrest in his report of this battle says: "The whole force charged down at a gallop, and I am proud to say that my men did not disappoint me; standing firm, they repulsed the grandest cavalry charge I ever witnessed. The Second and Seventh Tennessee drove back the advanced line, and as it wheeled in retreat, poured upon them a destructive fire. Each successive line of the enemy shared the same fate, and fled the field in dismay and confusion, losing another piece of artillery and leaving it strewn with dead and wounded men and horses."

This was one of the most terrific day's fighting ever experienced by the regiment; and night, which put an end to it, was rather welcome. After night, Capt. F F Aden, by direction of Gen. Forrest, sent Lieut. W B. Winston, of Company C, with about twenty-five men of that company, to keep up the appearance of pursuit, and allow the weary enemy no rest over night, which duty was performed by that accomplished officer with his usual vigor and energy The Federal retreat now became a panic, and was continued until rest and safety were found in the Federal lines at Memphis. The regiment's loss in this combat was 2 killed, 16 wounded, and 3 missing.

Gen. Forrest, in his report quoted above, further says: "I desire to testify my appreciation of the skill and ability of Cols. Robert McCulloch, R. M. Russell, and W L. Duckworth, commanding brigades. Col. Duckworth took command of Forrest's Brigade after Col. Forrest fell on the morning of the 22d ult."

February 23, the enemy being in rapid retreat, the regiment was ordered back to Starksville and thence to Mayhew's Station, where, on the 6th of March, it was transferred with the Twelfth, Fourteenth, and Fifteenth Tennessee Regiments (then at Grenada) to and constituted the First Brigade of Chalmers's Division, under Col. Richardson. The Seventh, however, remained with Chalmers for the present under command of Col. Duckworth, the remaining regiments being at Grenada under Richardson. About this time Capt. W F Taylor, who about a year previous had been detailed with his company, A, on special service with Brig.-Gen. W H. Jackson in other departments, re-appeared among his old comrades and was at once commissioned as lieutenant-colonel of the regiment by seniority The regiment had now a full complement of of field officers, to wit: Colonel, W L. Duckworth; Lieutenant-colonel, W F Taylor; Major, C. C. Clay; and Adjutant, W S. Pope.

On March 15, being on the march to Tupelo, the regiment was rejoined by the brigade, which was then placed under command of Col. Neely, *vice* Col. Richardson, who had been relieved from duty March 12.

The regiment was detached March 15, and with McDonald's Battalion (under Lieut.-Col. J. M. Crews) turned north-eastward, and was at Jackson, Tenn , on the 20th, and later at

Trenton and Humboldt; and on the 23d marched with Faulkner's and McDonald's Regiments, under Col. Duckworth, on Union City

About the 21st Capt. Aden's company, G, under that adventurous commander, was detailed at Purdy from the regiment on the march to escort Gov. Isham G. Harris, of Tennessee, to Paris, in that State. Marching rapidly in the prosecution of this errand, the company, about forty strong, came in sharp collision, near Mansfield, in Henry County, with a battalion of Federal scouts, and a hot combat ensued, the company losing two men wounded, and the enemy losing their major and another man killed and several wounded. Both parties retreated, the company having performed their duty of protecting their charge, and the Federals, it is supposed, imagining that they had encountered a large force. The company rejoined the command at Trenton, but too late for the Union City expedition.

Col. Duckworth, with his command, having reached the vicinity of Union City on the 23d, learned from a scout that there were no defenses there but rifle-pits, and determined to attack the position at daylight, the Seventh Tennessee and Crew's Battalion charging it on the north, and Col. Faulkner's command attacking from the south. The attack is thus described by Col. Duckworth: "The burning of a house by the Federals while it was yet dark revealed the fact that they were securely lodged in a strong fort and protected for hundreds of yards by a heavy abatis. This defeated our plan of attack. Our troops were dismounted, and under cover of the darkness were drawn close around the fort. After daylight some heavy skirmishing was had; meantime the colonel commanding decided, having no artillery, the post could not be carried by assault. What was to be done was the question.

"The colonel commanding determined to try the experiment of a ruse. He accordingly submitted his plan to the commanders. Col. Crews heartily concurred, but Col. Faulkner refused, saying he did not believe it would succeed. The colonel determined, however, to try it. The plan was to make the impression on the Federal commander that the long pause in the firing meant that we were waiting for re-enforcements. To strengthen this impression the horse-holders in the rear were to sound bugles and raise a loud cheer, which was taken up by the dismounted men in the bushes, who were to advance and resume a brisk fire; while this was going on the colonel commanding, at the head of a company of mounted men, dashed up under fire of the fort and remained for awhile as if making observations and then retired. The colonel then wrote a demand for immediate and unconditional surrender of the post, to which he signed the name of N B. Forrest, major-general commanding, and sent it under a flag of truce commanded by Lieut. H. J. Livingston. To this Col. J H. Hawkins, Federal commander, replied, begging time and saying that in the meantime he wished to see Gen. Forrest. This cornered us, for Forrest could not be produced. The colonel wrote another dispatch saying: 'I am not in the habit of meeting officers inferior to myself in rank under a flag of truce, but I will send Col. Duckworth, who is your equal in rank, and who is authorized to arrange terms and conditions with you under instructions. N B. Forrest, major-general commanding.' Col. Duckworth, at the head of Livingston's squad, handed Col. Hawkins the reply. After a lapse of five minutes, Hawkins handed to Duckworth a written surrender. Thus the Federal post, 300 horses, army stores, and about 475 prisoners, passed into the hands of about 320 Confederates, almost without the loss of blood or the smell of powder."

In a foot-note on page 469 "Campaigns of Gen. Forrest," we find it stated: "It is but justice to say that Lieut. W. S. Pope, adjutant of the Seventh Tennessee, and Lieut. W. M. McConnell, of Henderson's Scouts, by their presence of mind and intelligent conduct of the flag of truce, contributed largely to the success of the Confederates on this occasion."

Moving thence by way of Jackson, 30th, and Pocahontas, 31st, and back through Covington, the regiment was, April 12 and 13, during the attack by Gen. Forrest on Fort Pillow, occupied in observation at Randolph, seven miles below that point. It was thence marched to Brownsville, where it rejoined the brigade April 15, and was at Somerville on the 16th, and at Holly Springs on the 18th of April. From there they returned to West Tennessee to recruit and remount.

On May 2 the regiment (with brigade) was ordered to Tupelo under Gen. Buford as convoy for trains and prisoners, and were, May 4, at Rienzi, and at Tupelo on the 6th, where the brigade was returned to Chalmers's Division.

During this movement part of Companies E and L were still at Bolivar and vicinity, where they became involved in the skirmish which McDonald's Battalion, under Lieut.-Col.

Crews, had with the enemy on May 2 in front of Bolivar, Tenn. Four of Company E, who shall be nameless, had been on a lark that day, and the whole party were feeling strongly the inspiration of bold "John Barleycorn." When the command retreated through Bolivar these four youngsters "made a stand" in front of the residence of a well-known citizen, and quickly came in collision there with the head of the Federal column at not more than fifty yards' distance. The first volley sent the four horses rolling in the dust, when they quickly recovered their feet, but two of the youngsters, being top-heavy, could not remount their wounded steeds. They were lifted into the saddles by the other two, and the whole party rode off unhurt by the storm of bullets sent after them by the Federals, who were annoyed beyond measure at the contemptuous indifference of the well-soaked youngsters and the ineffectiveness of their own fire. They afterward declared that "the boys were bullet proof."

May 24 the regiment was with the Eighteenth and Nineteenth Mississippi Regiments organized as Rucker's Sixth Brigade of Chalmers's First Division, and was soon after, with the Nineteenth Mississippi, detached under Col. Duckworth on special service under Gen.

Lee at Grenada. May 29 the regiment was ordered back to the brigade, which was concentrated at Oxford, Miss.

While moving from Oxford to New Albany on June 5, Gen. Rucker was ordered to throw a portion of the brigade between Memphis and the rear of the Federal raid, then marching toward Tupelo, and capture his trains and cannon while pressing the Federal flank. This raiding party was in powerful force under Gen. Sturges, and was at Salem on June 4.

On June 6 Rucker's Brigade was ordered to hasten to New Albany and thence to Baldwin so as to make a junction with the main body of Gen. Forrest's command. Crossing with great difficulty at New Albany on the afternoon of June 7, and carrying their ammunition across on their horses, the Seventh Tennessee and part of the Eighteenth Mississippi were thrown upon a Federal brigade under Winslow, and drove them two miles until stopped by darkness. Next day the brigade was ordered to push on to Ripley on the Federal right flank and at Boonsville, on the 9th of June, effected a junction with Buford's Division.

Company B, Capt. Russell, having been detached on the 9th on a foraging expedition, encountered the enemy that day out toward Ripley in large force, and being fired upon, retired under a hill, throwing out skirmishers on the top of the ridge under Sergt. Nat Mason. These were assailed by the enemy and driven in, Sergt. Mason being killed. Privates Collier and Sale volunteered to recover his body, which they did under a hot fire without further injury than a shot through the clothing of Private Collier

On the 10th, moving before day by way of Old Carrollville, the regiment was in the vicinity of Baldwin in the forenoon. Ordered to move rapidly now to get in the enemy's front, who were advancing on an almost parallel road, the regiment, wearied from a sleepless bivouac in the rain, urged their tired horses along the muddy highway toward Brice's Cross Roads. Company G, Capt. Aden, being in the rear urging up the stragglers of the command. In the meantime Gen. Forrest, riding rapidly down from Boonville in advance of his command, reached Old Carrollville, and there learning that the enemy were but four miles from the Cross Roads, the objective point of his command, sent forward Lieut. R. J. Black, of Company B, then temporarily attached to his staff, with a few men of the Seventh to observe and report the movements of the enemy. Lieut. Black soon became involved in a skirmish with the enemy about one and a half miles north of the Cross Roads, and thus was the first to open the battle. Lyon's Brigade having been ordered up and become engaged with the enemy a short distance below the Cross Roads, the sound of the guns became apparent to the regiment on the march, and soon the order came to close up and move rapidly to the front. From this point the regiment rode in a gallop to the field on the left of Lyon's men, and dismounting in a skirt of woods, were immediately formed and marched into an open field, where they, with the Eighteenth Mississippi Regiment, went under fire and immediately prepared to charge the enemy. The latter occupied a wood on the far side of the field, with a thicket fence greatly strengthened with rails and logs and garnished with an abatis of such bushy trees as could be cut across the fence. In the field a deep gully ran parallel with the line of advance and this ditch bisected the regiment, which was formed across and on either side of it. It was now noon and very hot and sultry, when the order to charge was given. Instantly, as the regiment moved forward under Lieut.-Col. W. F. Taylor (Col.

Duckworth having been ordered to duty on another part of the field), the fence and abatis were ablaze with the fire of the enemy's breech-loaders, and the men began to fall thickly on the field. The fire was terrible from this invisible foe, and the regiment was staggered. The men began to drop upon their faces and seek shelter in the small gullies, when Lieut.-Col. Taylor, who was mounted, dashed down the line, ordering them up and calling upon them to go forward in the charge. Thus encouraged, the regiment, with loud cheers, rushed up the slope to the defenses of the enemy, leaving the ground strewed with fallen comrades in their rear Among the first killed was the gallant Adjutant W S. Pope, who against orders insisted on fighting mounted, and his horse was brought to Lieut.-Col. Taylor, whose own horse was killed in the charge. Reaching the enemy's defenses of brush and rails, the regiment hesitated, as there seemed no way of getting over the obstructions, and the enemy's fire was more deadly than ever at not more than forty feet range. But some one cried out, "Pull out a tree, boys," and with the vehement energy of battle some of the men in front of Company C seized one of the brushy-topped black-jacks in the abatis and pulled it bodily into the field. Through the gap thus formed, the regiment, shouting, poured pell-mell, and found themselves at once mixed up with the hitherto unseen enemy, and a deadly struggle at arms length began for the possession of the position. Guns, once fired, were used as clubs, and pistols were brought into play, while the two lines struggled with the ferocity of wild beasts. Never did men fight more gallantly for their position than did the determined Michigan regiment for the black-jack thicket on that hot June day An incident of the fight will illustrate its close and deadly character. Sergt. John D. Huhn, of Company B, being a few feet ahead of his company as they passed through the brush, came face to face with a Federal soldier, and having only an empty gun, he presented it at the blue jacket and ordered him to throw his gun down. This he promptly did; but several of his companions sprung to his rescue, and the sergeant avoided a bullet in his brain by wrenching aside the muzzle as the gun exploded. They then struck his extended carbine from his hand, breaking a finger and his arm in two places, and then laid him out by a terrible blow on his crown. Privates Lauderdale and Maclin, of Company B, then came to his assistance, shooting two of his stout-hearted assailants and driving the others off with clubbed guns.

Company G. Capt. Aden, having been, as heretofore stated, placed in the rear of the brigade on the march to the battle-field, did not reach the field in time to enter the battle with the regiment; but galloping into the skirt of woods whence the regiment moved under fire, shortly after the battle began, was there met by Col. Duckworth and ordered to go into the fight on the left of the regiment, which it did with great spirit, soon overtaking the regiment and taking part in the vehement charge on the fence and thicket. In this onset Capt. Aden was wounded in the hand and compelled temporarily to leave the field, but returned in time, late in the afternoon, to take part in the fight beyond Brice's house, at which part he was temporarily in command of the regiment, Lieut.-Col. Taylor having lost two horses during the afternoon, and being for the time prostrated by the heat and fatigue.

Color Sergt. A. H. D. Perkins, of Company E, the "unlucky," was, at the commencement of the fight, ordered by Col. Duckworth to remain with the horse-holders, as the fight promised to be largely in thickets and the flag liable to be torn to pieces, But seeing the charge begun, the sergeant's enthusiasm got the better of his discretion, and marching across the field he got in front with the old flag and, as usual with the luckless fellow, got a shot through the leg, being the fifth he had received in little more than a year.*

And thus the combat raged, the regiment steadily gaining ground, and together with the Eighteenth Mississippi, which had found lodgment on the left, in about two hours drove the enemy out of the woods and back to Brice's house, where their artillery was captured.

The fight was now, 2 o'clock P.M., general and terrific. Rucker, moving forward in the alignment, bore down all opposition, and the enemy at one time making a serious counter-charge and dashing up to within thirty yards of the regiment's front. But their line of near-

---

* Sergt. John D. Huhn, for this and other gallant and meritorious conduct habitually shown by him, was by Col. Duckworth promoted and appointed adjutant, vice Lieut. W S. Pope, killed in this combat. Col. Duckworth subsequently, in an indorsement upon an official document, thus speaks of Sergt. Huhn: "Applicant was assigned by me as within stated for distinguished gallantry on the battle-field and for his uniform excellent soldierly conduct. He is an excellent and most worthy soldier."

ly a mile in length was penetrated at all points. The enemy being finally driven across Tishomingo Creek, the men were remounted to pursue. Meanwhile Barteau's Regiment, the Second Tennessee, having gained their rear, they were thrown into great confusion and began to abandon their wagons, artillery, and all manner of property by the way-side. The pursuit was kept up five or six miles until stopped by darkness. Lieut.-Col. Taylor having stopped briefly from exhaustion, Capt. Aden was temporarily in command and had his horse killed. The pursuit was renewed shortly after midnight. One part of the regiment being led by Col. Duckworth, and another part by Lieut.-Col. Taylor, charging the enemy whenever they stopped to make defense, they were borne steadily back to Stubb's farm, where the regiment in the lead struck the enemy, who stampeded, leaving nine pieces of artillery and their wagons and wounded at a small branch of the Hatchie River. Thence they swept onward toward Ripley, near which place, in a charge, the gallant Capt. W. J. Tate, of Company E, and Privates Poindexter and T. R. Elean, of Company B, were killed. Lieut. W. B. Winston also greatly distinguished himself, as usual with that dashing soldier, in the pursuit, which was kept up until Salem was reached, and only ceased when the men and horses were too exhausted to go farther. In this affair the regiment lost 21 killed and 33 wounded, mostly in the charge across the open field at the outset. Among the wounded was the intrepid Capt. F F Aden, of Company G, shot in the hand, but not disabled.

Reaching Salem, the brigade was turned back to gather up stragglers and property, arms, accouterments, etc. The enemy had been defeated and driven fifty-eight miles in twenty-five hours, leaving behind all their trains, artillery, and wounded, and more than 1,600 prisoners. Altogether, considering the difference in numbers, this was the most remarkable cavalry victory of the war. The regiment was soon after, June 22, at Aberdeen, and June 30 at Verona, and on July 9 was thrown out four miles west of Tupelo to meet the grand movement under Gen. A. J Smith, which culminated in the battle of Harrisburg. On the 11th the regiment was at Pinson's Hill, two miles south of Pontotoc, on the Confederate left and on the Cotton Gin Road; on the 12th it was withdrawn several miles with the trains, and later in the day ordered back to the front; and on the 13th was marched across to the Tupelo road, twelve miles south-east of Pontotoc, and reached Barrow's Shop, on that road, about 3 o'clock P.M.

Here, moving under Gen. Chalmers in person, they were thrown upon the flank of the enemy, and for a time got possession of his train; but the enemy quickly concentrated upon them a furious fire of two regiments of infantry (Seventh Minnesota and Twelfth Iowa), and the men were soon driven from their prey, after having disabled eight wagons, two ambulances, and one caisson, which were burned by the enemy. The loss of the command in this brush was severe, including Maj. C. C. Clay, again dangerously wounded.

Hanging now on the Federal rear, the regiment bivouacked, after a hot day, within four miles of Tupelo, on the Chesterville Road. The brigade was so reduced by heat, and exhaustion of the men and horses, that it only mustered about 900 out of the 1,600 men belonging to it. The regiment had only about half its force of 570 men.

On the next day, in the battle of Harrisburg, the brigade was on the left center, between Bell's and Mabry's Brigades. The morning had been consumed in marching and countermarching, which under the July sun had greatly exhausted the men, and they were poorly prepared to make the terrible assault they were soon called upon to do. Finally in the blazing sun, in an open field, the charge was ordered. The brigade was ordered leftward to support Mabry, and with a loud cheer rushed forward, Col. Rucker leading the left and Gen. Chalmers the right of the brigade. On they went over plowed ground and through a corn-field across the enemy's front for nearly two thousand yards, while the enemy's works were ablaze with the fire of artillery and small arms. Then reaching the part of the line to be assaulted, the brigade charged up the steaming slope by the right flank, the men falling everywhere from the murderous fire of the enemy's infantry and fainting by dozens from the intense heat and thirst. On they staggered up to within sixty paces of the enemy's works, and having lost one-third of the men from wounds or exhaustion, the brigade, after their gallant commander was twice shot, fell back to shelter, Col. Duckworth succeeding Col. Rucker in command of the brigade and Lieut.-Col. Taylor taking command of the regiment. It was a deadly struggle; and though repulsed, the regiment splendidly sustained its renown won on so many hard-fought fields. In this engagement and the pursuit the regiment lost Capt. J P Statler, of Company E; Sergt.-Maj. C. N Claiborn, of Company B; and 74 men killed and wounded.

In the fierce charge Color Sergt. Egbert Shepherd, of Company B, was shot down. "Save the flag!" cried out the desperately wounded man, and a dozen men rushed forward to grasp and uphold the beloved banner, an unknown member of Company E reaching it first and holding it aloft during the remainder of the day.

After dark, Gen. Forrest, taking the brigade mounted, under Col. Duckworth, moved around to the enemy's left and drew up close under their works and encampment. Their outer line fell back, being driven rapidly by Duckworth's men three-quarters of a mile upon the main body, which at once opened in the darkness the most uproarious fire of musketry ever heard by the regiment; but as they overshot the command in the darkness, but little damage was done. The enemy, however, are reported to have fired on each other in the darkness, as their loss was more considerable than could have been inflicted by Duckworth's little brigade.

The 15th was spent in constant combat with

the enemy, who had begun to retreat; and on the 16th the regiment was ordered forward in pursuit, and skirmished lightly for two days to the vicinity of Kelly's Mills and New Albany

The regiment, when this movement began, July 10, 1864, had on its rolls for service 595 men, and at the close of the operations, July 17, 1864, only 433 men answered at roll-call, a reduction by death, wounds, or prostration of 162 men. More than half of these were killed and wounded in the several engagements. (MS. notes of Lieut. R. J Black.)

August 30, 1864, the regiment was by General Order No. 73, together with the Twenty-sixth Battalion, or Forrest's old regiment, and the Twelfth, Fourteenth, and Fifteenth Tennessee Regiments, all Tennessee troops, organized as a brigade, "to be designated as Rucker's Brigade," and by the same order Col. E. W Rucker was assigned permanently to the command of that brigade. (Official letter of Gen. Chalmers, September 12.)

This change created considerable dissatisfaction among the field officers of the brigade, not that they did not consider Gen. Rucker a brave and competent man, but they claimed that under army regulations the senior field officer of the brigade was entitled by seniority to the command. This dissatisfaction resulted in a correspondence with Gen. Chalmers, commanding the division, in which he censured the protesting officers and warned them that they were insubordinate in not cheerfully complying with General Order No. 73. But not noticing this warning, and refusing to obey the orders of Col. Rucker, on the 12th of August Cols. F M. Stewart, J. U Green, W L. Duckworth, J J Neely, and Maj. Phil T Allen were, by order of Gen. Forrest, suspended from their commands and placed under arrest, and next day Col. Duckworth was sent to Mobile. This left the regiment under the command of Lieut.-Col. W F Taylor, and it so continued until it assembled at Gainesville, Ala., to be surrendered in May, 1865.

CHAPTER IV

Again Off for Tennessee—Capture of Athens—Rich Spoils of War—Col. Taylor Wounded—Assault on Pulaski—The March to Columbia—Capture of Block-houses—Retreat from Tennessee—The Ruse at Newport Ferry—A Council of War—All Safely Across—The Johnsonville Raid—Capture of the Gun-boats—Service as Horse Marines—Destruction of Stores at Johnsonville—A Novel Scheme to Shoe the Horses—Hood's March to Nashville—Driving the Enemy's Cavalry—Assaults on Mount Carmel and Spring Hill—The Struggle at Franklin—Before Nashville—Deadly Conflict with the Enemy's Right Wing—Col. Taylor Saves the Regiment—The Fighting at Harpeth River and Richland Creek—Hardships of the Winter Retreat—Recrossing the Tennessee—Relief for the Starving Horses.

On September 1 the regiment was ordered to march from Oakland to West Point, there to embark for Mobile under orders from Gen. D. H. Maury; but at West Point, on September 4, received orders to come no farther.

By September 14 it had marched to Tupelo, and there halted until the 16th to draw rations and prepare for their long march "across the Tennessee," a movement which always brought more joy to the Tennessee troopers than any other occurrence of the war. On September 16 the grand forward march began, the brigade being temporarily under command of Lieut.-Col. D. C Kelley Moving by Mooresville, 16th; Marietta, 17th; Osborough, 18th; they crossed Bear Creek on the 19th, and encamped at Cherokee Station, on the Memphis and Charleston railroad and near the Tennessee River.

Every thing ready, the regiment rode to and forded the "Rubicon," the beautiful Tennessee, on September 21, at Colbert's Ferry, at the lower extremity of the Muscle Shoals, by a tortuous and dangerous ford one and a quarter miles broad. Moving across in closely drawn file, the command is described as resembling the "sinuous folds of a great serpent." Passing through Florence, Ala., on the 22d, and marching over a rocky, rough highway, crossing Shoal Creek seven miles east of Florence, they encamped about seventeen miles east of that place, and on the 23d reached the vicinity of Athens just before sunset, which place was strongly fortified and garrisoned, driving in the enemy's outposts and encampments to their fort. The regiment passed the night in a pouring, pelting rain, standing in line of battle south-east of the town. On the 24th it moved early through the outskirts of the town to a point almost eight hundred yards west of the fort, and was there posted in support of a battery About 12 M., a train arrived from Decatur with a strong detachment of infantry on board intended to reenforce the garrison, and this force left the train near a block-house about a mile from the fort. Col. Kelley promptly interposed his brigade, and at once the Seventh Tennessee was in serious collision with this strong force They were soon re-enforced by detachments of Wilson's, Logwood's, and Jesse Forrest's Regiments, and Nixon's and Carter's Battalions, and after an hour's hard fighting, the enemy threw down their arms and surrendered to the number of 400. In the meantime, at 1 P.M., the fort surrendered with its garrison of 1,400 men, and the two block-houses then yielded with garrisons of 85 and 35 men respectively, the smaller one, however. requiring an incentive in the shape of a few shells from Morton's guns, which killed and wounded several of the men. Moving at 5 P.M., the command marched toward Suphur Trestle, and encamped eight miles from Athens. At daylight on the 24th the men were in the saddle ; and after a ride of three miles, were dismounted and rapidly formed in front of the enemy's strong works at the Trestle. The brigade, charging across an open field led by Col. Kelley quickly came to the enemy's rifle-pits, two hundred yards in front of the redoubt, and drew up closely under cover of some bluffs and ravines around the enemy's intrenchments. The loss in this charge was 7. Col. Kelley's horse being shot under him. The place was now cannonaded, with the result of killing the Federal commander, Col. Lathrop, and about 200 of his men, when the redoubt surrendered with the remainder of its garrison of 820 men, mostly negroes, but including the Third Tennessee (white) Federal Cavalry. The command got here 2 pieces of artillery, 16 wagons, 700 stand of arms, and 300 cavalry horses, the latter a grateful sight to many badly mounted troopers in the Seventh. The succeeding incidents are thus given in Private J. J. Elean's diary:

Monday, September 26. — Our column was in motion at sunrise this morning, still proceeding up the railroad. Arrived at and burned the railroad bridge across the beautiful stream, Elk River, about 8 o'clock A. M. Here the enemy had a block-house, which we compelled them to evacuate by means of a flank movement so well designed by our commander Proceeded a few miles farther and burned a negro corral, where 2,500 negroes were employed on government farms. They had 600 acres of land in cultivation, and many fat beeves, which we sent south for the subsistence of our army Moved farther, and burned a very fine railroad bridge about seven miles south of Pulaski.

September 27 the brigade advanced toward Pulaski on a road parallel with the railroad. About six miles out the enemy attacked the advance, and for a short while drove them back. But the command moved steadily forward, fighting with determination the stubborn enemy, who were evidently stouter soldiers than those encountered at Sulphur Trestle and Athens. Three miles out from the town the enemy made a resolute stand. Kelley's Brigade was on the extreme left.

Gen. Forrest, in his report, says: "The engagement was becoming a general one The enemy threw his right around for the purpose of making an enfilading fire upon my troops, who had pushed far into his center About this time my troops on the left advanced, and the artillery in that direction unexpectedly opened a destructive fire, which caused the enemy to make a hasty retreat. He was closely followed up, and driven into town and into his fortifications."

The fighting had now (1 P.M.) continued hotly for about seven hours, and the regiment's loss was 7, including Lieut.-Col. W F Taylor, wounded. Capt. McCutchen, of Company H, took command of the regiment, which he held for the balance of this raid.

The command was now withdrawn, and went into camp in the vicinity; but after dark, leaving their camp-fires burning brightly, commenced a rapid march toward Fayetteville, on the Chattanooga railroad, but were stopped by a pouring rain after marching seven miles. At daybreak, on the 28th, the march was resumed, and continued to a point five miles beyond Fayetteville, where the command encamped, having marched forty miles that day. Lieut.-Col. Taylor, disabled by his wound, was left here to recuperate. Next day, September 29, the command was within fifteen miles of Tullahoma. Here the command was divided, and the regiment, with Lyons's and Bell's Brigades and McDonald's Battalion, went with Gen. Forrest toward Spring Hill.

Encamping near Petersburg on the night of September 29, they were at Lewisburg at noon on the 30th; crossed Duck River at Hardison's Ford, and were at Spring Hill at noon on the 1st of October. The march of the command on the 30th was forty miles, over the roughest and rockiest of roads in a wild country. On the 2d the command was in motion and menacing Columbia, encamping that night at Mount Pleasant; and on the 3d marched toward Florence, encamping within seven miles of that point on the 5th. Here Companies B and C, under Capt. J P Russell, were detached to convey the beef cattle direct to Colbert's Ferry, and the regiment marched before daylight to Florence, where the day and night of the 6th were spent in ferrying the wagons and artillery across the Tennessee River.

Concerning this week's movements the diary of Private J J Elean, of Company B, contains this narrative:

Saturday, October 1.—Left camp very early, moving in the direction of Franklin. After traveling in this direction for a short distance, turned toward Columbia. Passed through Spring Hill, a beautiful town, and came to the railroad again, tearing it up for many miles;

burned two wagons. Moving down the railroad in the direction of Columbia, we came to three block-houses. which surrendered to us with 138 prisoners after a brisk skirmish. By the capitulation of these block-houses we were enabled to burn several very fine bridges and about six miles of the railroad. After maneuvering considerably, we marched off by the very brilliant light of the burning road and block-houses, and camped eight miles from Spring Hill. The light could be seen from our camp.

Sunday, October 2.—Recrossed Duck River, moving in the direction of Columbia, near which place we arrived at about 2 o'clock P.M., driving in the enemy's pickets, which was followed by heavy skirmishing, in which we persisted but for an hour, losing 1 man killed and 2 or 3 wounded—had my horse shot. The enemy had a very formidable fort and a large force. We were withdrawn, and marched about six or seven miles on the Mount Pleasant road, and camped for the night.

Monday, October 3.—Passed through the beautiful little town of Mount Pleasant.

Tuesday, October 4.—Passed through Lawrenceburg, beyond which we camped on the Florence road.

Wednesday, October 5.—Great deal of rain last night. This morning we march for the Tennessee River Passed through Lauderdale Factory, on Shoal Creek, and camped six or seven miles from Florence

Thursday, October 6.—Crossed the Tennessee River at Newport. Commenced early in the morning and continued until the 8th inst., when all were over but about three regiments The Seventh Tennessee (with the exception of the First Squadron), the Second Tennessee, and Sixteenth Tennessee were prevented from crossing at this place by the enemy, who was steadily advancing with a largely superior force. Our squadron was detached on the night of the 5th inst., and was thus enabled to get over the river before the regiment came up.

Friday, October 7.—The First Squadron of the Seventh Tennessee crossed the Tennessee. The scene was indeed grand at night.

Saturday, October 8.—We left Cherokee Station and marched to Chickasaw Bluff in search of our regiment.

The crossing referred to above was difficult and dangerous, the river being high and the weather stormy, which so delayed the crossing of the command, with which was the main part of the regiment, that the enemy under Rousseau and Steadman were soon in close proximity, and making dispositions to surround and prevent the escape of their wily enemy and his little army. At this juncture, and while the enemy's bullets were beginning to splash in the water among the swimming troopers, the Second, the Seventh, and the Sixteenth Tennessee Regiments, and Winder's Battalion of Alabama Troops, all under Col. C. R. Barteau, of the Second Tennessee, were directed to retire on the Waterloo road. The ruse succeeded. The enemy followed in hot pursuit, when, at the crossing of Cypress Creek, the little rear-guard turned and stood at bay and disputed the passage with Steadman's Division. But, being flanked, they fell back, slowly fighting, on the Newport Ferry road.

Soon after, in conjunction with Col. Winder's, the Seventh, now under Capt. H. C. McCutchen, was ordered back on the Waterloo road, and fought steadily all day of the 9th, holding the enemy in check until the men and wagons of the command were safely ferried across. The regiment was then ordered to scatter and recross the river wherever possible. A council was called by Capt. H. C. McCutchen, in command of the regiment, on the receipt of this order; and it was agreed that each company commander should take his own company, and move in different directions, to embarrass the enemy and prevent pursuit, which was done. The several companies moving off sought the enemy's rear, and so effectually puzzled the enemy's commanders that they soon abandoned all search for them, and shortly began to retire. This left the roads to the South open, and the several companies soon turned their heads in that direction, the common object being to effect a crossing of the river This was safely accomplished at Newport Ferry by most of the command, on the 13th, without the loss of a man, and the regiment, with its consorts, was highly commended by the general commanding for its devotion and courage during this trying ordeal. Col. C R. Barteau, of the Second Tennessee Regiment, commanded these detachments north of the river which so successfully aborted the effort of the enemy to prevent the retreat of Forrest's command across the Tennessee.*

---

*Gen. Forrest, in his report, erroneously places Col. A. N. Wilson in command of these detachments. Col. Barteau was the ranking officer, and commanded the detachment.

During these operations Companies B and C, which had been detailed on the 5th, as above stated, reconnoitered the river below to intercept any effort by gun-boats to strike the command from that direction.

Leaving Chickasaw on the 9th, they were at Corinth on the 10th, Pittsburg Landing on the 11th, and again at Corinth on the 13th. On the 17th, the regiment still under Col. Kelley's command as a brigade commander, was on the march for Johnsonville, by way of Henderson Station and Jackson, Tenn., where, October 21, Col. Rucker again rejoined and took command of his brigade, which, together with Mabry's Brigade, was returned under Gen. Chalmers's command, and moved by the 24th to McLemoresville; and on the afternoon of the 29th it was at Paris, Tenn., and later at Paris Landing.

The regiment was rejoined on the 22d at Cotton Gin, near McLemoresville, by Company B, which had marched by way of Davis's Bridge, Matamoras, Newcastle, Wesley, and Brownsville, enjoying a short respite at Wesley

About noon of the 30th the regiment, having arrived on the bank of the beautiful Tennessee at Paris Landing, witnessed the unsuspecting approach of a transport, the "J W Cheeseman." The boat being allowed to pass the battery of light guns established on the river bank under cover, so as to bring it safely between the batteries at Paris Landing and those at Old Fort Heiman, was opened upon by the guns, and, being quickly disabled, had to surrender to Capt. Lawler, of Company C. The steamer proved to be laden with sutler stores and furniture, and the candies, nuts, and good things were quickly handed around and devoured by the hungry troopers, so long accustomed to hard-tack and lean beef.

Later in the day the regiment took part in the assault on the gun-boat "Undine" and the transport "Venus," which that morning had passed the upper batteries at Paris Landing, and found themselves entrapped between those batteries and the guns at Fort Heiman. Moving down the river with the artillery, being sections of Walton's, Rice's, and Martin's Batteries, the gun-boat was assailed; and after a noisy fight, was driven ashore disabled on the opposite side and abandoned. Having secured these boats, they were fitted up as a fleet, and manned with artillerists and troopers and soon moved down the river toward Johnsonville, the regiment moving along the shore in close company Lieut. I. N. Stinson, of Company B, with a detachment of 25 men, was on one of the steamers. Meeting the enemy's gun-boats, a fight ensued on November 1, in which the "Venus" was disabled and captured; and on November 2 the "Undine" shared the same fate, the "Horse Marines" being badly worsted in their first naval combat, and entirely willing to do all their riding "on a horse" thence afterward.

The regiment reached the vicinity of Johnsonville on the 1st, and took post with Mabry's Brigade about three miles south of that point, where they remained on the 2d; and on the 3d were established nearly opposite the point of attack; and on the 4th were interested observers of the destruction of the Federal stores, an immense pile, on the opposite bank by our artillery, and also of their gunboat and transport fleet by the artillery which had been pushed up by hand to within eighteen hundred feet of the enemy's position on the opposite bank.

On the 5th, after a farewell volley at a regiment of negro troops on the opposite bank, the regiment was withdrawn southward; and on the 6th were at Old Perryville, where they remained, "riding around," as stated by Lieut.

Black in his diary on the 7th; and on the 8th crossed the Tennessee in skiffs and flats, swimming their horses behind, a few of which were drowned.

Finding themselves now in a rocky country, and the horses being without shoes, the regiment was in a dilemma. They could not proceed, and to remain where they were would be fatal. But the fertile resources of the men of the Seventh were not long at fault. Visiting all the blacksmith shops in the surrounding country for miles, they obtained iron by stripping the tires from the farmers' wagons in the vicinity, and with the aid of the smiths in the command all horses were soon shod and ready for the road.*

Proceeding on the 9th by way of Linden, they were on the 10th at Ashland and Waynesboro, and on the 11th reached Hood's army at Florence, camping at the old mills on Cypress Creek. The regiment remained here until the 15th, when it marched in the afternoon to Gooseford, on Shoal Creek, where it remained until the 19th.

On the 16th the enemy drove in the pickets, but soon retired, and next day Company B relieved Company I on picket.

---

*MS. notes of Capt. F F Aden.

On the 18th the enemy in force assaulted the outpost, and a hot skirmish followed with varying fortunes, until 12 M., when the enemy retired; and the regiment following, obtained their forage to the northward of the scene of conflict, returning to camp that night.

On Sunday morning, November 20, the grand advance of Hood's army began. Lieut. R. J Black writes of the regiment's part in this movement in his diary as follows:

Sunday, November 20.—Left camp about midnight, moving only twelve or fifteen miles.

Monday, November 21.—Resumed march about 9 A.M., and camped again about three miles beyond West Point. In the meantime had considerable snow, and we all came near freezing. I never suffered so much before, for the length of time, with cold.

Tuesday, November 22.—Regiment moved out one and a half miles, procured two days' rations of corn, and returned to camp again. Still snowing, and very cold. Capt. Russell being sick. W N Hill was detailed to escort him into the country to rusticate for awhile.

Wednesday, November 23.—Left camp very early Marched rapidly in the direction of Columbia, via Henryville and Mount Pleasant. Driving the enemy pell-mell before us, arrived in front of Columbia about 8 o'clock A.M. of the 24th. Since leaving camp, traveled forty-two miles. Lieut.-Col. Dawson, of the Fifteenth Tennessee, killed, and one private of Forrest's Regiment, besides two or three of other commands wounded.

The fighting on the 23d was very severe. The brigade charged after dark in the direction of some firing, and nearly came in collision with a small force under Gen. Forrest; but the cheers of the men being recognized by Forrest, a dire disaster was avoided. The brigade lost during the day 5 killed and 30 wounded, including the loss in Forrest's escort, in whose company they were fighting.

In motion early on the 24th, by way of Mount Pleasant, the Federal rear guard was overtaken at Gen. Lucius Polk's place and forced back upon the works at Columbia. In this charge Lieut.-Col. Dawson, of the Fifteenth Tennessee, was killed; and Lieut. W B. Winston, of Company C, was seriously wounded in the forehead, the scar of which he still bears. Disposing the men, Col. Rucker commenced a steady skirmish with the enemy's pickets, which was maintained all the afternoon.

On the 25th Lieut. Black, with 20 men of

Company B, were detached as foragers, and did not rejoin the regiment until December 1.

On the 26th the brigade was encamped at Webster's Mills, ten miles south-west of Columbia; and on the 28th was ordered eastward to cross Duck River at Holland's Ford, seven miles east of Columbia, which was accomplished that afternoon; and after dark they *bivouacked* about four miles north of the river

Before day on the 29th the brigade moved forward on a rough, rocky country road toward Hurt's Cross Roads, and encountering the enemy early in the day, bore them back by sharp fighting to the Cross Roads. About noon an attack was here made by the three divisions of Buford, Chalmers, and Jackson, and the Federals were forced back to Mount Carmel Church. In this day's advance Company A, Seventh Tennessee, which had so long been absent from the regiment, and was still detached as escort to Gen. Jackson, formed the van-guard, and made several dashing charges on the Lewisburg and Franklin turnpike, in one of which Private F M. Nelson engaged a Federal trooper with his saber, and was knocked from his horse by a blow from the "blue jacket's" blade. The gallant Federal was instantly killed, however, by a shot from the pistol of Private J. M. Tate, who had come to his comrade's rescue.

At Mount Carmel another fierce attack was made on the enemy's works and rail-piles, which were carried by storm in a beautiful charge of Jackson's Division; and the whole command turned sharply to the left, and, after a rapid gallop of five miles, came on the enemy's infantry at Spring Hill, and the regiment took part, about sundown, with the infantry under Cleburne in the assault on the works. This assault was successful, the enemy being driven out of the intrenchments into the town, and after dark the regiment was drawn back, and bivouacked in the immediate vicinity.

On the 30th the regiment was dispatched west of Spring Hill to the Carter's Creek turnpike to guard the Confederate left flank, and that afternoon drove in the Federal pickets on the extreme left at Franklin. Establishing the brigade within a few yards of the enemy's intrenchments, Col. Rucker maintained a hot skirmish with their outer lines until night, while the main attack was made by the infantry on the right. The enemy having evacuated Franklin on the night after the deadliest conflict in which our army was engaged during the war, the Confederates losing over 6,000 men in less than two hours, the regiment on the next day was thrown north-westward to the Hillsboro and Nashville pike, and followed that highway without obstruction to the vicinity of Nashville, where they arrived December 2, when the regiment formed in line of battle in front of the town, the skirmish line being posted about three miles from the city

On the next day the regiment was ordered around to the left wing of the army, and was soon engaged in animated skirmish with the enemy in the vicinity of the Charlotte pike, which lasted all day

On Sunday, December 4, the enemy opened heavily upon them with artillery, which continued all day, while the crack, crack of the skirmishers' rifles kept time with the deep pounding of the big guns. There was no child's play in front of the Seventh Regiment during this investment of Nashville. It was constant deadly work, bringing into play all the nerve and coolness of the veterans to maintain their position in front of their powerful and persistent foe. On one occasion Company B of the regiment, being left well advanced on the picket line at night, was lost sight of during some changes in the position of the regiment, and when wanted could not be found. They were supposed to be captured, but Sergeant A. L. Elcan, volunteering to look for them, found the company right on the enemy's line, and sheltered from destruction only by the friendly blackness of the night. They escaped without loss.

December 6 the regiment was marched down the Charlotte pike several miles to the Cumberland river, to observe the enemy's movements on that stream, and were by 10 o'clock A.M. in sharp collision with one of the Federal gun-boats, which came down from Nashville to pay its respects. At 2 P.M. the regiment was in line of battle on the river front, to meet some more gun-boats which had appeared, and, after enduring considerable shelling, the boats retired. On the next day the regiment was moved nearer Nashville, on the Charlotte pike, and on the 8th relieved Kelley's Regiment (McDonald's battalion) on the skirmish line.

The weather was growing rapidly colder and very disagreeable to the troopers, and on the next day (9th) a snow-fall added nothing to their comfort. The regiment was withdrawn a short distance, leaving one company (B) on picket. On Sunday (11th) the regiment was forced close up to the enemy's skirmishers, and remained that day in line with horses saddled, enduring the bitter cold as best they could; and thus they remained on the 12th and 13th, Company G being on the skirmish line in the afternoon of the 13th. The weather next day turned warmer, and a thaw set in.

December 15 will never be forgotten by the men of the Seventh. At 10 o'clock in the morning the enemy's skirmishers, in clouds, came pouring over the hills and through the valleys, and soon became hotly engaged with their attenuated antagonists. They were held in check, however, in the regiment's vicinity, until 2 P.M., when the left wing of the infantry were brushed back by the onset on the Hardin pike, and the cavalry under the gallant Rucker were thrown back toward the Cumberland River, and entirely cut off from the army Here the enemy made a desperate effort to capture the regiment, a strong force following hotly in its rear, and a still larger one moving rapidly forward on its left flank (*en retreat*) to try and get in its rear The moment was a perilous one, but Lieut.-Col. Taylor, notwithstanding the confusion of the rush to escape this flanking fire, halted, and formed successive squadrons fronting the flanking enemy, and would fire upon them, sometimes at only a few paces distance, and then fall back until again overtaken by the flankers, when they would repeat this maneuver. This saved the regiment, and, once rid of this persistent flanking movement, the men were again formed in line of battle, and retired slowly, fighting every step back to the Donelson place, seven miles from Nashville on the Charlotte pike, from which place at midnight they withdrew across to the Hardin pike, near the left flank of the army, and encamped.

Next morning betimes the regiment was moved over to the Hillsboro pike, near the Brentwood hills—the extreme left of the Confederate army—and remained here in the immediate presence of the enemy until 3 P.M., when it was ordered farther down the Hillsboro pike, toward Franklin, with orders to picket that flank of the army, which was now in full retreat. Here, at day-break on the 17th, Companies B, D, and E, constituting the picket front, were assailed by the enemy in great force, and compelled slowly to retire; and at noon, having rejoined the regiment, the whole force were formed on the Franklin pike, but were soon driven headlong into Franklin.

Here the Confederate infantry had formed, and, supported by some artillery, held the enemy in check; but, a flanking force appearing to the left rear of the regiment, now in the rear of that flank of the enemy, the regiment retreated across the Harpeth; and, moving rapidly to Spring Hill, encamped. At the crossing of the Harpeth the enemy charged with great impetuosity in the dark; and a small party, consisting of Lieut.-Col. W F Taylor, Lieut. R. J. Black, Private Jack Somerville, and another private whose name is not remembered, found themselves separated from the command and in the immediate presence of the enemy But it was a life and death struggle now, and this little squadron held their ground, emptying their revolvers right in the faces of the enemy at a few paces, and then retired safely across the river without injury to one of them—an almost miraculous escape. On the 18th the remnant of the brigade, including the Seventh Tennessee, moved out to the Carter's Creek pike, where they burned three railroad bridges, and at Rutherford Creek three more, and encamped about five miles from Columbia, on the Carter's Creek turnpike. On the next day they held the line of the creek to the left of the infantry, skirmishing heavily, and at dark moved into and encamped at Columbia, about 10 P.M. of one of the coldest nights of the war. The cutting wind and bitter cold were almost unendurable, even by the hardy veterans who had undergone so much exposure before on that dreadful winter retreat.

December 20 the regiment moved out to Gen. Pillow's farm to feed, and returned to encampment near Columbia. It was sleeting, and freezing to every thing, and bitter cold. Next day it moved through Columbia, and marched eastward up Duck River, picketing it for some distance above town. On the 22d a detachment of the enemy effected a crossing in front of the Seventh Tennessee pickets, showing a very grave negligence on the part of some persons unknown, and the regiment was immediately retired toward the Pulaski turnpike; and the rear guard, composed of eight fragmentary brigades of infantry, 1,600 strong, under Walthall; 1,200 cavalry, under Jackson; 500, under Chalmers; and a few hundred, under Buford, commenced falling back in the forenoon. The Seventh encamped for the night at Bigbyville; the infantry and Jackson's Division several miles to the northwest and above Lynnville. On the next day the regiment retired by Campbellsville to Bordenham and encamped, being posted in observation on the left flank of the retreating army. Moving on the 24th, early, toward Lynnville, the regiment took part on the left flank in the bloody fight of the rear-guard, at Richland Creek, just south of Lynnville. Assailed here by overwhelming numbers, Chalmers and Buford, whose joint command did not exceed eight hundred men, were pressed back vehemently across Richland Creek, just west of the bridge on the Pulaski pike. At this moment Company A, still on detached service, had been ordered by Gen. Forrest to burn the bridge, and about a dozen members of the company were engaged in that duty when the general charge was made by the Federals. Making a run for their horses, the men on the bridge were saved from capture by Gen. Jackson, who halted two guns of Morton's battery, and opened with canister on the pursuing column of the enemy. Regaining their horses, the remnants of Chalmers's Division, including the Seventh, were now observed running down the wooded slope on the left, beyond the creek, and, crossing over, seemed to be fighting hand to hand with the enemy in the open field on the south side of the stream. Jackson's Division was now again pressed into the fight, and the onset of the enemy was checked. Just before crossing the creek, while in line in support of the artillery, Company A lost their gallant lieutenant, H. W Watkins, his thigh being crushed by a cannon-shot from the enemy's battery He lived but a short time after he was hit. He was one of the bravest men in the regiment, and had been mentioned by his commander specially for gallantry and daring at Corinth and other places.

The regiment, under Lieut.-Col. W F Taylor, was now moved through Pulaski, and on Christmas-day was posted on the left flank at the fierce struggle at Anthony's Hall, and the next day again took part in the final repulse of the enemy at Sugar Creek. From thence they marched undisturbed to the Tennessee River, at Bainbridge, crossing that stream on the pontoon bridge on the night of the 27th; and after floundering in the mud for some time, and losing many horses bogged down in the morass, the regiment encamped after daylight. On the 28th it proceeded to Barton Station, twelve miles west of Tuscumbia. The weather was again extremely cold.

The regiment moved on the 29th to Iuka,

MAJ C C CLAY

CAPT J P RUSSELL

COL W L DUCKWORTH

LIEUT H J LIVINGSTONE

PRIVATE JAMES FENTRESS

crossing Town Creek on the railroad bridge, and moved next day to Burnsville. In this march the horses were nearly starved from want of corn, some of the regiment being without corn except two small feeds for four days.

On the next day, in the afternoon, they marched to Burnsville through a cold, pelting rain.

Resuming the march on December 31, the regiment moved to Corinth, and next day to near Rienzi. The horses had had only three feeds since crossing the Tennessee, and the country afforded nothing. But late in the afternoon of January 2 a full supply was received. The horses were so frantic from hunger that many of them almost choked themselves to death with their halters when they got sight of the welcome corn.

CHAPTER V.

Temporary Consolidation — The Regiment Furloughed—A Rush for Home—Return of the Men to Camp—The Regiment in Convention—Patriotic Resolutions—The Wilson Raid—March to Alabama—Conflicts at Scottsville and Centerville—The Last Gun—Announcement of the Surrender—Grief of the Men—Dividing the Old Flag—A Sad Farewell.

ON January 3 the Seventh Regiment, reduced by the vicissitudes of the late campaign to a mere handful of mounted men, was, together with the Twelfth, Fourteenth, and Fifteenth Tennessee, and Kelley's Regiment (Twenty-sixth Battalion), consolidated, and remained in camp near Rienzi next day, being addressed at dress parade by Col. Kelley

Here a great and delightful surprise awaited the war-beaten veterans. On the 5th of January, about 8 A.M., they were marched into Rienzi and notified by Gen. Chalmers that they were as a body furloughed for twenty days, and could in that interval go where they pleased. Loud shouts of joy burst from their lips, and with three cheers for their esteemed commander, Gen. Chalmers, the command, without further preparations or ceremony, turned their horses' heads by companies toward their homes in West Tennessee.

The rush and hurry of that ride for home, through the blinding snow-storm, will never be forgotten by the participants, many of them riding from fifty to sixty miles per day, so as not to lose an hour of precious time. And then the joyous fleeting hours at home, where the weather-beaten, battle-scarred troopers reveled in the delights of sunny smiles and joyful tears of tender mothers and sisters, and lived on all the good things that the pitiless war on the border had yet left in the larders. But time seemed to fly with eagle wings, and the time too soon came to return to camp and hardship. To their lasting honor be it said, the old Seventh to a man returned to their colors. Some lingered by the cozy firesides of home, and were a few days late, but all came back; and in a few weeks after their furlough the regiment—remounted, re-clothed, and imbued (from association with the patriotic ladies in old Tennessee) with freshened zeal for the cause—were in better condition for service than they had been for many a month before. Nearly all the stragglers and dismounted men of the late campaign had returned, and the regiment was now ready to take part in the final struggle for independence, which was soon to occur in the prairie regions of Central Alabama.

The regiment remained quietly in camp, now at Verona, for several days refitting and shoeing horses; and on February 21 held a mass-meeting to give expression to their determination to fight to the bitter end the common enemy. This meeting was presided over by Surgeon C. K. Caruthers, with Lieut. O. S. Rice and Sergt. John W Shelton as Secretaries.

The Committeee on Resolutions were Capts. L. W Taliaferro, F F Aden, and C. H. Jones, Lieut. H. F Sale, and Corp. W T Ulyrick.

Addresses were made by Capt. Taliaferro and Lieut. H. J. Livingston and others.

The Committee on Resolutions reported, with appropriate preambles, the following resolutions, which were adopted, and are here given in part as illustrative of the spirit of the regiment at that late period of the war:

1. *Resolved*, That we have every confidence in our ability to defeat the efforts of our enemy, expel his armies, frustrate his purposes, and ultimately gain liberty and independence.

2. That, as we value our rights and institutions and the long-cherished principles of our government, we are still resolute and determined to fight for them to the last, and risk our all in their defense.

3. That we are determined to gain our independence, and to rely upon our arms until it is achieved; and we counsel our people and comrades to take courage and fresh resolution; and we do invite our citizens to co-operate with us to encourage our men to come to the field, and to discourage desertion, to raise supplies for our armies, and to give all aid and support to the common cause. And we appeal to the fair women of the South to continue to employ their influence in behalf of their beloved country; to continue to merit the praise and honor awarded them by our brave soldiers for their devotion and fidelity to our cause, and for the patience, constancy, and fortitude with which they have adhered to it; and we earnestly beseech them to discountenance and frown upon those of our countrymen who have deserted our cause, or refused to come to its defense in this hour of peril.

The following additional resolutions were offered by Lieut. Livingston, and unanimously adopted:

Resolved, That in the impending struggle for national independence our whole available resources should be brought into the field; and we view with a mingled feeling of pity and contempt that class of so-called Confederate officers and soldiers (more properly styled "non-combatants") who cowardly hide themselves behind "bomb-proof" positions far in the rear, and who are ever ready to hear the news from the front, and criticise the movements of our generals upon the field; and the thousands of others who, to avoid the dangers incident to the regular service, are resorting to the guerrilla service, committing every character of depredation upon our citizens, and briging shame and disgrace upon our noble cause; and we earnestly call upon our authorities to use every practicable means to abate this nuisance.

The following was offered by Capt. F F Aden, and adopted:

Resolved, That, although we are not fully convinced of the expediency of enlisting and arming slaves for the service, we will, nevertheless, cheerfully acquiesce in the policy of our government upon the subject, whatever that may be; and at the same time, are fully persuaded that they might be made available otherwise in strengthening and rendering more efficient the armies which have been so long submitted to the privations, hardships, and even menial positions of the camp and field. We would, therefore, respectfully call the attention of our President and Congress to the practicability of relieving with this element details of able-bodied men, already made from the ranks, as the teamsters, cooks, etc.; and for further providing for the comfort and efficiency of white soldiers by furnishing them with such servants as they actually need for the performance of those menial services which, in addition to the regular duties of the soldier, frequently become onerous and exhausting.

The following was offered by Corp. E. S. Austin, and unanimously adopted:

Resolved, That we look back with honest pride upon the achievements of this cavalry corps within the last twelve months under the command of our noble chieftain, Maj.-Gen. Forrest, and do again pledge him our hearty co-operation in his every effort to drive the hireling from our beloved country.

About March 1, 1865, the regiment was assigned to Brig.-Gen. A. W. Campbell's Brigade in Jackson's Division; and on March 17 was at West Point, Miss. On March 27 the regiment was put in motion for Selma to meet the "Wilson Raid."

On the 28th the regiment was at Columbus; on the 29th at Pickensville; on the 30th at Tuscaloosa; and on the 31st encountered La Grange's Brigade eighteen miles from Tuscaloosa, and, after a slight skirmish with that command, rested on their arms. Early on April 1 the command again attacked them to the north of the Tuscaloosa and Scottsville road (a part of Company A being in the fight), and bore them back for fifteen miles up the mountain road, prostrating many of the horses in the regiment and brigade. After the chase, the enemy (except a few troopers) escaping, the regiment moved back toward

Scottsville by a short road, and about dark encountered Croxton's Division eight miles north of Scottsville. After a skirmish both sides bivouacked; and about daylight the Confederates again assailed Croxton at the junction of the Scottsville and Tuscaloosa roads, and drove him rapidly, after a sharp fight in a lane, into and through Scottsville and onward to Centerville, on the Cahawba, over which stream the bridge, after a stout effort to prevent them, was burned by the enemy From the opposite bank they then threw a few shells at three members of Company A, who were sitting on their horses a half-mile away, which were the last guns fired at the regiment during the war.

The war was now practically over.

In a few days Lee surrendered at Appomattox, and then Joe Johnston at Goldsboro. On the 26th of April Gen. Dick Taylor surrendered the troops in his department, and the regiment was marched to Gainesville, Ala., to be paroled.

When the determination of the commander was made known to the men, they were bowed down with unutterable grief. The strong men who had thrown themselves with the fiery energy of Rupert into the vortex of battle, who had hurled back the charge at Prairie Mound, penetrated the serried lines at Tishomingo Creek, and breasted the sleety storm from the intrenchments at Harrisburg now drew back in terror from the ignominy of passing under the conqueror's yoke, though it were to peace and rest beyond. They gathered in groups under the forest-trees at Gainesville, and in low tones told of their despair. Many wept like children. Then came reaction; a sudden fever seemed to seize the men. There were their arms and horses. They would go to the Trans-Mississippi Department and continue the struggle for Southern independence. But Gen. Forrest said: "No." What could not be accomplished here could never be done in the thinly settled West. Again despair seized the men. But they soon became calm as they realized the hopelessness of their cause; and, with the grim determination which had carried them so gloriously through the war, they decided to go home and to face the consequences, whatever they might be. But the old flag—bullet-torn and dim, whose blue cross had been triumphantly borne aloft for years at the cost of so much blood and valor—they would never part with that.

On the eve of surrender, as the shadows of night fell, the men reverently gathered round the staff in front of regimental head-quarters, and, tearing the silk into fragments, each concealed in his jacket, next his heart, a bit of the coveted treasure. The flag had been the gift of a young lady of Aberdeen, Miss., made from her dress, and had never for an instant been abandoned by the men of the Seventh after it was committed to their guardianship.

On May 11 the men received their parole, a copy of one of which is here given as follows:

No. 68.   GAINESVILLE, ALA., May 11, 1865.

Private John P Young, of A Company, Seventh Cavalry Regiment Tennessee Volunteers, C. S. A., residing in Memphis, Tenn., having been with the approval of the proper authorities paroled, is permitted to return to his home, not to be disturbed by the United States authorities so long as he observes his parole and the law in force where he may reside.

By order of Maj.-Gen. E. R. S. Canby, U. S. A.

E. S. DENNIS,
Brig.-Gen. Vols. Com. for U. S.

This paper contained the following indorsement:

I certify on honor that Private John P Young is in good faith the true owner of one horse.

J. W SNEED,
Captain Commanding Company.

These paroles were universally observed by the men with the same soldierly sincerity that distinguished them during the war; and all the survivors are to-day, so far as known, honorable, and not a few of them distinguished citizens of a happy and reunited country

The men, by the terms of their paroles having been allowed to retain their horses, which, under the organization of the Confederate cavalry were their own property, at once prepared to start for home. Ten men of Company A volunteered to remain with Gen. W H. Jackson, Commissioner on the part of the Confederate authorities for paroling the troops, in order that he might not be deprived of proper and needed assistance in his duties, and the remainder of the regiment, after many a sad farewell and friendly grasp of the hand as old comrades parted, turned their horses' heads homeward, and for the last time rode out of camp.

Thus, on May 12, 1865, ended the career of the Seventh Tennessee Cavalry

CHAPTER VI.

DETACHED SERVICE OF COMPANY A UNDER GEN. JACKSON.

In the spring of 1863 Company A, still on detached duty as an escort to Brig.-Gen. W H. Jackson, went with that commander to Central Mississippi, where during that summer they operated in conjunction with Gens. Pemberton and Joe Johnston's command, in the vicinity of Vicksburg and Jackson, and along the line of the Big Black River. The men were constantly exposed during this campaign to arduous courier and picket duty. From there they went with Gen. Jackson to Georgia, and took part in the campaign against Sherman in his march to Atlanta. To write a complete narrative of the movements of the company during this period would require almost the space occupied by the foregoing history of the regiment, and will not be attempted here. From the Atlanta lines the company accompanied Hood on his march to the Tennessee River, going by way of Cedartown, Ga.; Gadsden, Asheville, and Blountsville, Ala., to Tuscumbia. The succeeding events occurring during the disastrous raid of Hood's army into Middle Tennessee, and the terrible winter retreat from Nashville, will be given in greater detail.

On November 10, 1864, the company, arriving from Georgia with Jackson's Division, crossed the Tennessee River at Tuscumbia Landing, and went into camp at Florence, about a mile from town, on the old military road or Indian trail. Here it remained encamped and getting ready for the coming campaign, until November 20. Jackson's Division was here merged again with Gen. Forrest's command, and the company for the first time in nearly two years came back into the same command with the regiment. Though not again amalgamated with the regiment, it was destined from this time to the close of the war to serve in immediate company with their old commander, Lieut.-Col. Taylor. On November 20 the movement into Tennessee by Hood was begun; and the company, habitually in advance with their general, took an active part in all the movements of that terrible and disastrous campaign. While doing duty as an escort to General Jackson, it was often actively engaged with the enemy; and the men individually, as daily detailed for courier duty, suffered much from exposure, but had a splendid opportunity of witnessing all the grand tactics of that wintery struggle, amid the rocky hills and valleys of Middle Tennessee.

November 20 the company took the road northward toward Lawrenceburg, in a cold, steady rain. On the same night the weather began to change, and on the 21st made good roads by reason of the hard freeze. On the 22d the company rode into Lawrenceburg in the evening behind the charging columns of Armstrong's Brigade, and complacently made their supper off the abandoned rations of the retreating Federals, still simmering on the campfires. Remaining here next day, on the 24th they moved north-eastward to Campbellsville, and took part in the assault on Hatch's Division at that place in the afternoon. Just as the Federal retreat began the company, which was supporting a section of Young's Battery in plain view of the enemy, was ordered to charge, and immediately rushed headlong down the long slope in line. No enemy was seen by the men, but several were supposed to be out toward the left flank in the direction it was charging, and the men went forward with great spirit, but were soon recalled. No casualty occurred, except the fall of Private John Marton from his horse. The company then followed the retreating Federals, camping that night near Campbellsville. The men next day made a long march to Columbia, and camped at the Granville Pillow place, near that city. Remaining here until the 27th on the skirmish line, the company was marched eastward several miles, to Fountain Creek; and on the 27th moved rapidly to Hall's Mill, on Duck River, which it forded under a skirmish fire from the opposite bank, many of the horses swimming. Then, turning eastward again, the men were in immediate contact with the enemy all the way to the Lewisburg and Franklin turnpike, where the enemy were attacked and driven off from the ford by Ross's Brigade, of Johnson's Division. After nightfall a brigade of the enemy, which had been cut off at the ford, made an attack suddenly on the men of Ross's command, who, unaware of their presence, were cooking supper. It was a genuine surprise, and Privates Matthews, Young, and Watts, of the company, were caught by the head of the Federal column and borne back nearly a mile between two rock fences before they could shake off their unwelcome visitors and escape into the field. Next day the company was in the advance, all day, of an exciting chase, and near Hunt's Cross Roads made a dashing charge on the enemy's rear for a mile. This brought up suddenly before some rail-piles. Part of the company made a detour here, while the remainder stood for half an hour under the fire of the enemy's skirmish line without firing a gun, a pretty severe strain. Private F M. Nelson, of the flanking party, soon after became entangled in the enemy's mounted pickets, and was severely hammered with a saber by one of them, who was at length shot and killed by Private James Tate with a pistol.

At Mount Carmel Church the enemy again made a stand behind rail-piles, but were driven off by the three divisions of Gen. Forrest's command, and the pursuit recommenced toward Spring Hill, to the westward five miles, the company still in the advance. At the latter place the pursuit was brought to a stand in front of the enemy's infantry, under Gen. Stanley, whom Hood's command was attacking. At midnight the enemy retired, and the company being on the right flank, resumed the pursuit in the darkness. About 4 P.M. the next day the company came out in front of the enemy's line at Franklin, and formed immediately in the rear of Loring's Division of Stewart's Corps. When, a few minutes later, that command moved forward in the charge, the company was galloped rightward to a ford over Harpeth River, and there took part in the attack on the defenses of the enemy's left flank north of the river An hour later, when Jackson's Division, out of ammunition, retired across the Harpeth, the company was, by order of Gen. Jackson, formed at the ford by Gen. Frank C Armstrong, and ordered to hold the position against all comers. The enemy's infantry advanced, but did not attack, evidently unaware of the weakness of the little squadron at the ford, and the army was saved from a serious flank movement in the darkness.

Next day (December 1) the pursuit was recommenced at dawn, and the company was kept well up in advance. About noon the company, in conjunction with Ross's Brigade, was pushed on the enemy's rear and subjected to a severe shelling by a battery, which they received, mounted, without breaking or retiring an inch—an unusual stand for cavalry At night it came alongside a big Federal encampment, who were foraging in a corn-field, and came near being entangled in the enemy's lines unawares; but the latter, catching the alarm from the firing of some scouts, hastily mounted and moved into Nashville. Next day (the 2d) the company moved up in plain view of Nashville, and for several hours watched the reduction by Morton's guns of some block-houses on the Chattanooga railroad.

December 3 and 4 the company remained in camp on the cold, snow-covered hills, and on the 5th was marched to Murfreesboro, being detailed that afternoon to receive charge of the surrendered fortalice at La Vergne, with the 80 prisoners captured there.

December 6 the company remained in camp near Murfreesboro and the Nashville pike. December 7 the company took part in repulsing the sortie of the enemy, and later were ordered to form in the rear of Bate's stampeded men, on Hurricane Creek, and assist in checking their flight. The next six days were spent in camp near William Bass's place, four miles from the town. The weather was bitter cold.

December 14 the company marched around Murfreesboro to the Shelbyville pike, and was engaged in the maneuvers and skirmishes in that quarter; and the same night stood guard for the division in front of a force of the enemy working along the railroad from Chattanooga, which was captured before day by Ross's men, with a railroad train which they were guarding. On the next day the men were engaged in maneuvering and skirmishing with a force of the enemy from Murfreesboro coming to the relief of the captured train. All day the men heard the guns at Nashville, and grew very anxious about the result of the battle. The company, in the evening, was marched rapidly back to the northward of Murfreesboro, and encamped near the Wilkerson turnpike. At midnight it was aroused by the news of Hood's defeat at Nashville, and an hour later commenced, in the bitter cold and sleet, the mournful retreat toward Columbia. The following three days were days of terrible exposure and suffering. The infantry, in large part, were barefooted and the cavalry scantily provided with clothing; and no one who took part in it will ever forget that terrible retreat by way of Triune and Eaglesville to Columbia, where it was hoped to get in with Hood's beaten army before they crossed Duck River. This was happily accomplished, and the company, half frozen by the terrible cold of the night of December 19, safely crossed the river and encamped at Warfield's, four miles south of Columbia. Here they remained until December 22, when, the enemy having forced the passage of Duck River, the rear-guard under Forrest, and consisting of 1,600 infantry and 1,200 cavalry, commenced falling back. The company was in the rear during the long retreat which followed to the Tennessee River, and suffered the greatest hardships and privations, being reduced to not more than 15 men for duty by the exigences of that terrible winter march and combat. Falling back slowly before the enemy, and fighting incessantly, Forrest kept Thomas's grand army in check for six long wintery days.

On the 24th the company was engaged in the combat at Richland Creek, and a detail of eight men being made by Gen. Forrest to burn the bridge over that stream, came very near being captured, and only escaped the charge of the mounted enemy by a tremendous run on foot for half a mile. Just north of the creek, in the afternoon, the company lost the gallant Lieut. Henry W Watkins, who was struck down by a cannon-shot while standing in front of the company The same shot cut off the leg of Private George Rainey's horse. Camping that night in Pulaski, the company moved out next morning, and in the afternoon took part in the fierce combat at Anthony's Hill, which was disastrous to the enemy. Marching all that night in the sleet and rain, over icy roads, the company crossed Sugar Creek at dawn, and a few minutes later watched the disastrous and final repulse of the enemy by the infantry on the banks of that stream. Another day's march brought them to the Tennessee River, which the company crossed on a sleet-covered poonton bridge at midnight of December 27, and by morning were at rest at the little village of Bainbridge, Ala. The sufferings of the men from hunger and exposure during that terrible retreat cannot be described, and the heroism and endurance of the little rear-guard surpassed the story of Napoleon's retreat from Moscow. The company then proceeded by easy marches by way of Tuscumbia, Burnsville, Saltillo, and Tupelo to Verona, Miss., where, on January 25, 1865, they were furloughed for two weeks to revisit their homes, and remount and refit.

Re-assembling at Verona by February 15, 1865, the men remained here in camp for some days, and after a short march to the vicinity of Saltillo to meet a supposed Federal raid in that quarter, the company went to West Point, Miss., where Gen. Jackson was placed in command of the "Tennessee Division" of Lieut.-Gen. Forrest's Cavalry Corps; and the company, after a separation of more than two years, was returned into the same division with the regiment, being still on duty as an escort or courier company for Gen. Jackson.

Toward the last of March the company accompanied the division in its march down into Alabama to meet the "Wilson Raid," then moving by way of Montevallo upon Selma, the Confederate depot of supplies and munitions of war. Moving by way of Columbus, Pickensville, and Tuscaloosa, the company took part with the regiment in the skirmishes with La Grange's and Croxton's Federal commands at Trion, Scottsville, and Centerville; and marching to Marion on the next day, overtook the remnants of Gen. Forrest's command escaping from Selma. The last guns fired at the regiment during the war were some cannon-shots fired at several members of the company by a Federal battery across the Cahawba River at Centerville, April 2, 1865.

After short encampments at Greensboro, Eutaw, and Sumterville, Ala., the company assembled with the regiment at Gainesville, where, on May 12, 1865, they were surrendered and paroled. Most of the men left at once for their homes, a few remaining with Gen. Jackson, who was the Confederate commissioner to complete the paroling of the men of Forrest's command at Gainesville, and afterward at Columbus, Miss.

ROLL

COMPANY A.

NOTE.—The names frequently mentioned on the roll as absent without leave, were not deserters, but only those who under indulgent discipline would absent themselves a short time and return. The deserters from the regiment are not embodied on this roll. Having voluntarily deprived themselves of the name of soldier, no notice is taken of them. The entries on these rolls under the head of " Remarks " are copied *verbatim* from the original muster rolls now in the archives at Washington.

Name.	Rank.	Date of Enlistment.	Remarks.
Thomas H. Logwood	Captain.	May 16, 1861	Afterward Colonel Fifteenth Tennessee Cavalry.
W. F. Taylor	Captain.	May 16, 1861	Wounded at Pulaski September 27, 1864. Afterward Lieutenant-colonel Seventh Tennessee Cavalry.
J. W. Sneed	Captain.	May 16, 1861	Wounded and mentioned for gallantry at Corinth by Col. Jackson October 5, 1862. October 31, 1863, on thirty days' furlough.
Thomas Howard	1st Lt.	May 16, 1861	Resigned in 1861.
H. W. Watkins	1st Lt.	May 16, 1861	Killed at Richland Creek, Tenn., December 24, 1864.
J. H. Wilburn	2d Lt.	May 16, 1861	October 31, 1862, absent. Wounded at Coldwater September 9, 1862.
W. L. Certain	2d Lt.	May 16, 1861	
E. B. Trezevant	Bvt. 2d Lt.	May 16, 1861	Afterward Lieutenant-colonel Tenth Tennessee. Killed at Thompson's Station, Tenn, May 5, 1863.
John D. Mitchell	Bvt. 2d Lt.	May 16, 1861	
H. P. Wooslar	1st Serg.	May 16, 1861	August 5, 1863, thirty days' furlough.
G. A. Stovall	2d Serg.	Aug. 12, 1862	Absent, scout duty, August 31, 1863.
W. G. Richardson	3d Serg.	May 16, 1861	August 5, 1863, thirty days' furlough.
John F. Graham	4th Serg.	May 16, 1861	

Name		Date of Enlistment	Remarks
H. F. King	1st Corp.	May 16, 1861	Captured near Memphis September 15, 1863.
W. H. Rollins	2d Corp.	May 16, 1861	November 9, 1861, on special detail twenty-five days.
A. J. Ivey	3d Corp.	May 16, 1861	
W. W. Shouse	3d Corp.	May 20, 1862	October 30, 1862, on duty as courier.
J. W. Fairburn	4th Corp.	May 20, 1862	
W. E. Matthews	4th Corp.	May 16, 1861	October 26, 1863, forty days furlough.
Tom Dye	4th Corp.	Dec. 9, 1863	
H. L. Farmer	Bugler	May 16, 1861	June 30, 1864, no horse.
Jerry O'Mara	Blacksmith	May 16, 1861	June 30, 1864, no horse.
J. E. Roberts	Farrier	May 16, 1861	Detailed to Medical Department February 1, 1863.

Privates.

Name	Date of Enlistment	Remarks
Ayres, Ike H.	Sept. 1, 1863	
Armstrong, T. W.		Wounded at Franklin March 31, 1863.
Alston, J. C.	July 29, 1861	Discharged October 26, 1862.
Anderson, James A.	Mar. 21, 1862	Detailed to raise company October 1, 1862.
Anderson, George	June 6, 1862	Detailed with Captain Anderson October 10, 1863.
Alexander, Jack		Wounded at Franklin March 31, 1863.
Boteler, W. J.		
Bynum, W. J.	Aug. 28, 1862	Wounded at Coldwater, September 9, 1862.
Burton, Frank	Mar. 21, 1862	Detailed with Captain Anderson October 16, 1862.
Bagby, W. M.	May 16, 1861	On special detail twenty-five days from November 9, 1863.
Bailey, J. S.	May 16, 1861	
Bragg, H. T.		
Bowe, R. B.	July 21, 1861	Detailed Assistant Commissary Subsistence Department September 25, 1862.
Breck, C. H.	Oct. 21, 1863	

Name	Date of Enlistment	Remarks
Bantyn, G. O.	May 16, 1861	Wounded at Coldwater September 9, 1862.
Bernard, A.	Aug. 22, 1862	Detailed in Assistant Quartermaster's Department Sept. 25, 1862.
Bloydes, B. W. C.		Wounded at Britton's Lane August 31–September 1, 1862.
Brinkley, S. B.	May 16, 1861	Detailed Assistant Commissary Subsistence Department November 23, 1862.
Cayce, R. E.	May 16, 1861	Wounded at Coldwater September 9, 1862, and discharged.
Carnes, R. S.	May 16, 1861	
Chambliss, F.	July 29, 1861	
Clarkson, G. (Rod)	Aug. 20, 1862	Wounded at Coldwater September 9, 1862.
Clayton, J. J.	Sept. 19, 1861	Wounded at Holly Springs December 20, 1862.
Christian, W. V.	Oct. 24, 1863	
Calla, Joseph	Sept. 1, 1861	Detailed in Assistant Quartermaster's Department September 1, 1863.
Chum, W. C.	May 16, 1861	Detailed with Capt. Anderson October 16, 1862.
Cox, Robert W.	May 16, 1861	Killed at Britton's Lane September 1, 1862.
Cummins, J. C.	May 16, 1861	
Capps, C. J.	Oct. 31, 1862	Detailed with Capt. Anderson October 16, 1862.
Cannon, H. E.	May 16, 1861	Detailed with Capt. Anderson October 16, 1862.
Dockery, D. M.	Sept. 25, 1862	June 30, 1864, absent on surgeon's certificate.
Dye, T. W.	Dec. 9, 1863	Afterward Corporal.
Davis, W. B.		Discharged; furnished substitute.
Eames, W. H.	May 16, 1861	October 31, 1862, detailed in Assistant Quartermaster's Department, as forage master, by Maj. Paul.
Edmondson, E. A.	Sept. 8, 1862	August 31, 1862, absent on duty, as courier.
Eaton, —.	Dec. 9, 1861	
Fuller, John	May 16, 1861	
Fairburn, J. W.	May 16, 1861	Afterward Second Corporal.
Farmer, H. L.	May 16, 1861	Division Bugler.
Freeman, E. B.	Mar. 24, 1864	

Fulgham, A. G.	May 16, 1861	
Fulgham, Tom	May 16, 1861	
Fleming, J. C.	May 16, 1861	Wounded at Paducah in October, 1861; Orderly Sergeant.
Graham, Joseph	May 16, 1861	
Graham, J. T.	May 16, 1861	Afterward Fifth Sergeant.
Graham, John	May 16, 1861	Killed at Holly Springs December 20, 1862.
Gale, J. A.	May 16, 1861	Furlough, thirty days from November 16, 1863.
Greenlaw, W. E.	Oct. 3, 1861	December 31, 1863, absent on surgeon's certificate since Sept. 15, 1863.
Graves, John	Aug. 20, 1861	
Henning, James		Killed at Holly Springs December 20, 1862.
Harris, Tom (Crow)		Transferred and killed.
Hurt, Milton		Killed with saber at Coldwater September 9, 1862.
Hill, A.	May 25, 1864	Captured near Collierville February 25, 1864.
Hillsman, J. T.	Sept. 15, 1861	Detailed to Medical Department February 7, 1863.
Henderson, J. L.	May 16, 1861	Wounded at Britton's Lane August 31–September 1, 1862. Detailed with Captain Anderson October 16, 1862. In Ordnance Department August 1, 1863.
Holmes, A.	July 29, 1862	Captured near Horn Lake January ——, 1863.
Holmes, N.	July 29, 1862	Captured near Jackson, Miss., July 9, 1863.
Holmes, Frank	May 16, 1861	
Holmes, George E.	May 16, 1861	On special detail twenty-five days November 9, 1863.
Holmes, Dr.	May 16, 1861	Wounded at Paducah in October, 1861.
Herron, L. A.	Aug. 14, 1861	October 31, 1863, absent on recruiting service.
Hazel, J. M.	Sept. 26, 1862	
Holeman, W. P.	Oct. 22, 1862	Detailed to Assistant Commissary Subsistence Department Jan. 1, 1863.
Hildebrand, J. J.	May 16, 1871	
Hill, W. C.	May 16, 1861	
Harris, Will R.	May 16, 1861	Transferred.
Harris, George C.	Sept. 25, 1862	Transferred. Captured near Memphis October 31, 1862.

Name.	Date of Enlistment.	Remarks.
Harris, West	May 16, 1861	
Hunter, ——	May 16, 1861	
Hogg, G. A.	July 29, 1861	Afterward Surgeon Company A. Sent to hospital Sept. 28, 1862.
Harrison, Isom	May 16, 1861	Sent to hospital September 28, 1862.
Harrison, J. R.	May 16, 1861	October 31, 1862, detailed with Capt. Slover.
Hall, W. A.	May 16, 1861	
Irwin, R. C.	May 16, 1861	
Ivey, A. J	May 16, 1861	Afterward First Corporal.
Jones, J. C.	May 21, 1862	Afterward Lieutenant and Aid-de-camp on Gen. W. H. Jackson's staff.
Jackson, L. K	May 16, 1861	December 27, 1863, on furlough.
Jackson, J. F	May 1, 1863	November 9, 1863, special detail twenty-five days.
Johnson, R. F.	Dec. 25, 1863	
Jones, Wiley F	Sept. 9, 1861	Detailed with Capt. Anderson October 16, 1862.
Jones, Arthur	May 16, 1861	
Jones, Norman C	May 16, 1861	October 19, 1862; absent sick.
Kendrick, J. A	Sept. 25, 1862	Wounded at Corinth October 4, 1862. Wounded at Franklin, Tenn., April 10, 1863. Died at Tuscaloosa, Ala., April 29, 1864.
King, H. F.	May 16, 1861	Died in prison. Captured near Memphis September 25, 1863.
Kilgore, John	May 16, 1861	Killed at ——.
Lane, Gus	May 16, 1861	Absent with leave October 31, 1864.
Lea, J. M	Aug. 25, 1864	
Long, W. H.	Aug. 1, 1863	
Lane, J. W.	June 14, 1861	
Lane, A. C.	May 1, 1864	
Lane, Judge		
Locke, Robert	Mar. 21, 1862	Detailed with Capt. Anderson October 16, 1862.

Name			
Locke, Charles		Dec. 3, 1861	Detailed with Capt. Anderson October 16, 1862.
Martin, J. H.		May 16, 1861	Detailed October 15, 1862, to assist the A. A. G.; afterward Aid-de-camp to Gen. Jackson.
Mitchell, H. P.		May 16, 1861	
Matthews, W. E.		May 16, 1861	Afterward Fourth Corporal.
Martin, John		May 16, 1861	
		Oct. 20, 1863	October 31, 1863, in hospital at Canton.
Mitchell, H. P		June 6, 1862	October 31, 1862, absent on parole. Captured at Denmark, Tenn., October 1, 1862.
McGowan, E. L.		Aug. 18, 1862	November 9, 1863, special detail twenty-five days.
McGowan, C E.		Aug. 18, 1862	Sent to hospital September 28, 1862.
McKnight, J. M.		May 16, 1861	Leave of absence, surgeon's certificate, thirty days from Oct. 20, 1863.
McCorkle, Thomas		Feb. 16, 1863	Captured June 30, 1864. Detailed to Assistant Adjutant General's office September 5, 1865.
Mills, J. B		May 16, 1861	Wounded at Coffeeville December 4, 1862.
McCullers, A. C.		May 16, 1861	October 31, 1862, absent, wounded accidentally.
Meyers, Charles		May 16, 1861	
McCallum, D.			
McCallum, John F.		June 16, 1862	Wounded and disabled at Coffeeville December 4, 1863.
Murphy, W. P.			
Nevens, W. S.		May 16, 1861	October 31, 1863, on duty as courier.
Nelson, F. M.		July 1, 1863	Detailed Assistant Commissary Subsistence Department Aug. 1, 1863.
O'Meara, George		May 16, 1861	
O'Meara, Jerry		May 16, 1861	Company blacksmith.
Owen, J. H.		May 16, 1861	
Patterson, W. L.		May 16, 1861	Detailed Assistant Quartermaster April 1, 1863.
Pickhard, J. H		May 16, 1861	
Poston, F. N		Aug. 18, 1862	Absent without leave after January, 1865.
Profit, T. J		May 16, 1861	Wounded at Franklin March 31, 1863.
Pruden, J. L		June 6, 1861	Wounded at Coffeeville December 4, 1862.

Name.	Date of Enlistment.	Remarks.
Paul, W. P	May 16, 1861	
Peyton, Vol.	May 16, 1861	
Pope, W. S.	May 16, 1861	Afterward Adjutant. Killed at Tishomingo Creek June 10, 1864.
Potter, Thad.	May 16, 1861	Wounded at Holly Springs December 20, 1862.
Rodgers, Frank.	May 16, 1861	
Richardson, W. G.	May 16, 1861	Afterward Second Sergeant.
Rodgers, Ford.	May 16, 1861	Absent, special leave fifteen days, November 10, 1863.
Rollins, W. H.	May 16, 1861	Afterward Fourth Sergeant.
Robson, E. D.	May 16, 1861	
Radcliff, T. D	May 16, 1861	Detailed to Medical Department August 31, 1863.
Rainey, J. N.	Mar. 20, 1862	
Rainey, George	Nov. 1, 1864	
Ragland, F. D.	Aug. 20, 1862	Wounded in Armstrong's raid, Medon or Britton's Lane, August 31, September 1, 1862. Hospital at Brandon July 20, 1863. Captured near Memphis in May, 1864.
Roberts, J. E.	May 16, 1861	Detailed to Medical Department February 1, 1863.
Rainey, J. M.	Jan. 20, 1865	
Rives, John	May 16, 1861	
Reviere, J. M.	Oct. 6, 1861	Wounded in charge at Franklin March 5, 1863.
Starnes, E. B	May 16, 1861	Killed at Franklin March 5, 1863.
Slover, A.	May 16, 1861	Absent without leave.
Sexton, Dennis	Aug. 13, 1862	Afterward Third Sergeant.
Stovall, G. A.	May 20, 1862	Afterward Third Corporal.
Shouse, W. W.	May 16, 1861	
Sangster, Samuel	Aug. 20, 1862	On duty as courier October 31, 1862.
Smither, C. G	May 16, 1861	
Snees, Albert	Mar. 21, 1862	On courier duty October 31, 1862.
Selden, M. L.		

The Seventh Tennessee Cavalry. 159

Name	Date	Notes
Selden, C C	Aug. 31, 1863	
Stevens, A. B	Aug. 27, 1863	Detailed to Medical Department June 25, 1864.
Stockell, C H	Sept. 1, 1864	
Tate, J. W	Jan. 6, 1861	Wounded at ———.
Tate, T. S.	Oct. 6, 1861	Detailed with Gen. Forrest May 30, 1863. Absent on duty for company October 31, 1862.
Treadwell, R. A	Oct. 7, 1861	On courier duty October 31, 1862. Transferred August 16, 1863.
Treadwell, B. D	Oct. 4, 1861	On duty as courier October 31, 1862.
Treadwell, E. M	June 6, 1862	Wounded at Medon or Britton's Lane August 31, September 1, 1862.
Thomas, T. J	Sept. 25, 1862	Wounded and disabled at Medon October 30, 1862. Discharged July 1, 1863.
Thomas, E. W	Oct. 4, 1861	Furlough thirty days November 7, 1863. Detailed to Transportation Department June 1, 1864.
Talley, F D	Oct. 28, 1862	
Talley, F H.	Oct. 28, 1862	Detailed to Transportation Department January 1, 1863.
Thomas, Phil.	May 16, 1861	Wounded at Medon October 30, 1862.
Tate, T. G.		
Trent, John.	May 16, 1861	Detailed with Capt. Anderson Oct. 16, 1862, and became Lieutenant.
Treadwell, R.		
Upshaw, Tim L	Aug. 14, 1861	Discharged October 26, 1862.
Walton, R. L.	June 3, 1863	In hospital at Canton October 31, 1863.
Watt, W. C	Nov. 1, 1863	
Watt, S. H.	Jan. 1, 1863	
Witherspoon, S. P	Sept. 25, 1862	Special detail twenty-five days from November 9, 1863.
Wooldridge, O.	Feb. 1, 1863	
White, Alonzo C	May 16, 1861	Killed at Oxford, Miss.
Wicks, Joe J	May 16, 1861 (?)	Detailed as Adjutant October 31, 1862. Killed at Oxford, Miss. December 2, 1862.
Wilburn, James H	May 16, 1861	Mortally wounded at Coldwater September 9, 1862, then Lieutenant.
Young, J. P	Nov. 1, 1864	
Young, John	May 16, 1861	Killed at Chewalla, Miss., October 3, 1862.

Total number enrolled, 200. Killed, 12; wounded, 27.

Company B.

Name.	Rank.	Date of Enlistment.	Remarks.
C. H. Hill	Captain.		Afterward Major, Logwood's Battalion. Wounded near Covington, Tenn., while a prisoner.
J. P. Russell	Captain.	August 23.	Promoted to Captain May 22, 1862.
J. U. Green	Lieutenant.		Afterward Colonel Twelfth Tennessee Cavalry.
R. A. Fidd	Lieutenant.		
H. T. Sale	Lieutenant.	October 4.	Promoted to First Lieutenant May 22, 1862.
P. T. Winn	Lieutenant.		Resigned November 21, 1862.
I. N. Stinson	Lieutenant.	August 13.	Captured at Lamar, Miss., November 8, 1862. Promoted to Brevet Second Lieutenant May 22, 1862.
R. J. Black	Lieutenant.		Wounded at Lockridge's Mill, Tenn., May 5, 1862; Hernando, Miss., June 16, 1863; Union City, April 24, 1864.
A. L. Elcan	Sergeant.		Wounded at Prairie Mound February 22, 1864.
James A. Wardlaw	Serg.	July 22.	August 31, 1862, absent, sick, since December 2, 1862.
J. R. Somerville	Serg.		Killed at Brice's Cross Roads June 10, 1864.
R. H. Harper	Serg.		Killed at Brice's Cross Roads June 10, 1864.
M. W. Hilliard	Serg.		
J. M. Myers	Serg.		
A. M. Elmore	Serg.		
S. A. Burkhart	Corporal.	July 9.	Absent without leave August 1, 1863.
J. B. Pollen	Corporal.		
T. F. Archer	Corp.	May 31.	Absent, sick since Sept. 1, 1862. Died April 30, 1863.
R. P. Archer	Corp.	May 31.	Absent without leave August 1, 1863.
R. E. Rogers	Color Serg.		
L. J. O'Kelly	Corporal.		

Name.		Date of Enlistment.	Remarks.
S. C. Chambers	Corporal.		
E. O. Sale	Corporal.		
W. A. Collier	Corporal.		

Privates.

Name.	Date of Enlistment.	Remarks.
Adkins, J. L.	March 18.	Absent without leave May 1, 1862.
Anderson, ——		Detached on duty with Gen. W. H. Jackson.
Banks, John D	July 9.	May 12, 1864, absent with leave. Killed near Nashville Nov. 1, 1864.
Banks, William H	May 31.	Absent without leave April 18, 1863.
Barden, N. S.	March 18.	August 31, 1863, absent without leave since December 3, 1862.
Bass, J. C		Transferred July 15, to Company "I," and mortally wounded at Harrisburg July 14, 1864.
Brown, Joe		August 31, 1863, absent without leave since November 10, 1862.
Beasley, T. J	May 31.	August 31, 1863, detached as Assistant Surgeon on Gen. Loring's staff January 28, 1863. February 29, 1864, detached as Assistant Surgeon on Gen. Loring's staff.
Blaydes, J. E.	August 13.	August 31, 1863, absent without leave since December 16, 1862.
Boylan Weldon	June 10.	Died at Camp Beslin of measles in 1861.
Bradshaw, S. G.		Absent with leave May 12, 1864.
Black, W. F.		
Benson, George	March 18.	Died August 28, 1862.
Bradshaw, W. M	May 31.	
Bunn, T. H.	March 18.	Transferred to Company K August 25, 1863. Afterward Second Corporal.
Chambers, S. C		August 31, 1863, detached for duty at regimental head-quarters December 30, 1862. Afterward Sergeant-major, December 31, 1863; and killed at Harrisburg July 14, 1864.
Claiborne, C. N.	May 31.	

Name.	Date of Enlistment.	Remarks.
Claiborne, J. M.	March 18.	April 30, 1863, discharged.
Coffield, John R.	March 18.	Transferred from Company K December 11, 1862.
Cocke, J. D.	August 13.	August 31, 1863, absent without leave since November 20, 1862.
Cocke, Tom		
Cockrell, J. A.	May 15.	Absent without leave one month from August 1, 1863. May 12, 1864, absent sick. August 31, detached on other duty since November 20, 1862.
Cothran, F. G.	May 31.	August 31, 1862, absent without leave since November 6, 1862.
Crenshaw, C. C.	May 31.	Absent without leave Aug. 1, 1863. Absent with leave May 12, 1864.
Culbreath, J. M.		April 30, 1863, on detached service. Wounded at Brice's Cross Roads June 10, 1862.
Collier, W. A.	February 15.	Afterward Fourth Corporal. Absent sick May 12, 1864.
Dillahunty, W H		Transferred from Company K.
Driver, S. P.		
Dillahunty, James	June 12.	Killed at Britton's Lane September 1, 1862.
Dickason, William		
Elean, J. J		Afterward First Sergeant. Wounded at Prairie Mound, Feb. 22, 1864.
Elean, A. J.		Afterward Fifth Corporal. Detached April 30, 1863.
Elmore, A. M.		Absent with leave, May 13, 1864. Killed at Brice's Cross Roads, June 10, 1864.
Elean, T. R.	March 18.	Absent, sick, May 12, 1864.
Elean, H. H.		
Field, John B.		
Flowers, James H		Taken prisoner while at home sick in October, 1862. Detached April 30, 1863.
Ford, J. E.	May 31.	Made Quartermaster Sergeant October 31, 1863. Detached as Assistant Forage Master October 21, 1862.
French, John A.	March 18.	August 31, 1862, on duty with Gen. Richardson's Partisan Rangers.

French, H. J	March 18.	Detached assistant blacksmith December 20, 1862.
Field, R. A.		Discharged at reorganization June 10, 1862.
Fraser, E. I		
Garrison, James L.	March 10.	August 31, 1863, transferred from Company H, Balch's Battalion.
Gee, James L.	May 31.	Absent without leave August 1, 1863.
Gibbs, G. R.	May 31.	(April 30, 1863, detached for other duty; August 31, 1863, absent, sick, since June 5, 1863.
Griffin, Lewis W	March 18.	Detached to get clothing August 31, 1863.
Goodman, W. V.	May 31.	Absent, sick, May 12, 1864.
Goss, John.	May 31.	Detached to get clothing August 31, 1863.
Hindman, J. C	July 9.	Discharged September 10, 1862.
Herron, W. S.	June 20.	Detailed as wagon master November 16, 1862.
Hill, W. N.	July 9.	Absent without leave May 1, 1862.
Hilliard, W. C.	March 18.	Absent without leave August 20, 1863.
Holloway, W. H.	May 31.	October 31, 1862, absent, sick; and August 20, 1863, without leave.
Hunt, James F		Disabled from attack of measles, at Columbus, 1861.
Hunt, John H.	March 18.	Detailed as druggist November 1, 1862.
Hambleton, O. E.	March 18.	Absent with leave May 12, 1864.
Hanner, Robert.		
Harper, Charles M.	July 9.	Discharged December 15, 1862.
Harper, Jack.		Killed in personal difficulty in 1862.
Harper, R. A.	July 9.	Absent without leave May 20, 1862.
Harris, Polk		
Hilliard, Tom.		Killed at Harrisburg July 14, 1864.
Hill, J. C		
Holloway, Daniel T.	May 31.	Discharged August 27, 1862.
Hilliard, John A.	July 9.	Discharged February 18, 1863.
Hilliard, M. W.	May 31.	Absent without leave August 1, 1863.
Jackson, C. E.	Nov. 10.	Absent, sick, May 12, 1864.
Jackson, G. W.	May 31.	April 30, 1862, detached on other duty; absent without leave February 11, 1863.

Name.	Date of Enlistment.	Remarks.
Jackson, J. P.		
Jackson, W. H.	Oct. 4.	April 30, 1863, detached on other duty; absent without leave January 24, 1863.
Jordan, C. W.	July 9.	Absent without leave December 17, 1862; also August 29, 1863.
Jordan, Thomas A.	March 18.	Absent, sick, January 31, 1863.
Johnson, W. A.		
Ligon, B. H.		
Locke, John A.	May 31.	Absent without leave May 20, 1862.
Loving, H. W.		
Lauderdale, D. N.	March 18.	Absent without leave December 23, 1862.
Lauderdale, James.		
Macklin, W. E.	May 31.	Discharged June 10, 1862.
Macklin, James N.		Absent without leave February 11, 1863.
Macklin, John S.	Sept. 22.	Absent without leave May 20, 1862.
Marklann, G. S.	May 31.	Absent without leave February 11, 1863; sick May 12, 1864.
Mason, W. N.	May 31.	Detached April 30, 1863.
		Detached on special duty January 17, 1863; killed near Brice's Cross Roads June 9, 1864.
McCall, M. S.	July 9.	Discharged April 30, 1863.
McClennan, K. B.		Absent, sick, November 14, 1862; without leave July 1, 1863.
Montague, A. W.	Oct. 4.	Absent, sick, September 20, 1862; without leave April 30, 1863.
Myers, James N.	Oct. 4.	Absent without leave August 1, 1862.
Maclin, John T.		Afterward Fourth Corporal. Wounded at Harrisburg July 14, 1864.
Maclin, W. F.		
Mason, R. E.		Discharged June 10, 1862.
Mason, F. Y.		
McNeely, T. B.		
McIlwain, R. G.	March 88.	Discharged October 18, 1862, being under age.

McIlwain, N. J. C.	July 9.	Discharged September 22, 1862.
Newton, James G. W.	March 18.	Absent without leave August 1, 1863.
Nobles, George W.	August 13.	Absent without leave May 12, 1864.
Nolley, Samuel Y.	Feb. 2.	Absent without leave December 6, 1862; also August 20, 1863. Absent with leave May 12, 1864; killed at Brice's Cross Roads, June 10, 1864.
O'Kelly, L. J.		Afterward First Corporal.
O'Connor, John.	May 31.	Discharged October 20, 1862.
Payne, John W.	July 9.	May 12, 1864, absent with leave.
Poindexter, L. H.		Captured near Egypt Station, Miss., February 29, 1864.
Poindexter, C. C.		
Poindexter, C. C., 2d.		Died in Kentucky.
Peppin, ——.		
Payne, R. H.	Sept. 1.	{ Left his regiment (Eighteenth Mississippi Infantry), sick, on May 28, 1862; and not being able to join his regiment, was ordered to this command.
Rice, J. M.	May 31.	Absent without leave December 23, 1862.
Rogers, R. S.	May 31.	Detailed to get clothing October 31, 1863.
Sale, F. O.		Afterward Third Corporal. Detached April 30, 1865.
Sale, G. B.		Wounded at Harrisburg July 14, 1864.
Sanford, Bailey.	May 15.	Absent without leave August 1, 1863.
Seay, C. I.		
Smith, John F.	August 13.	{ Absent, sick, in October, 1862. Captured at Old Lamar November 8, 1862. Wounded at Harrisburg July 14, 1864.
Sheppard, Egbert H.		{ Color-bearer. Transferred February 10, 1862, to Company L. Wounded at Collierville October 11, 1863. Wounded at Harrisburg July 14, 1864.
Somerville, A. C.		{ October 31, 1862, absent on furlough. October 31, 1863, detached. May 12, 1864, absent without leave.
Strange, W. H.		Captured at Old Lamar November 8, 1862. Absent, sick, Jan. 31, 1863.

Name.	Date of Enlistment.	Remarks.
Somerville, James R.	.. ..	Killed at Brice's Cross Roads June 10, 1864.
Somervell, J. W	.. ..	Afterward Adjutant of Seventh Tennessee, and Assistant Adjutant-general to Gen. W. H. Jackson. Killed in Atlanta, Ga.
Stevens, S. R.	.. ..	
Shivers, J. A.	.. ..	
Stone, J. I.	May 15.	Transferred, July 15, 1862, to Company 1.
Treadwell, G. W.	August 15.	Detailed to get clothing August 31, 1863.
Timons, B. F.	March 18.	Detached April 30, 1863.
Tobin, Pat	..	
Townsend, George W.	August 15.	Detailed to get clothing October 31, 1863.
Tucker, John T.	August 15.	Detailed April 30, 1863. On detail to get clothing August 31, 1864. Absent without leave May 12, 1864.
Treadwell, R. A	..	
Treadwell, A. C.	..	Absent without leave September 20, 1863.
Thomas, I. A.	May 31.	Discharged October 22, 1862.
Turnage, J. N	July 9.	Fourth Corporal August 31, 1862. Absent with leave since February 2. Detached to First Tennessee Cavalry April 30, 1863.
Walk, T. B.	August 13.	Wounded at Harrisburg July 14, 1864.
Wallace, William.	..	Sick February 29, 1864. Absent without leave April 1, 1864.
Watson, C. T.	..	Absent without leave November 20, 1862.
Wells, R. H.	..	
Westmoreland, A. G.	.. ..	Died from natural causes in camp.
Westmoreland, A. E.	..	
Westmoreland, W. J.	March 18.	Absent without leave December 7, 1862.
Williams, John F.	August 13.	Absent without leave December 30, 1862.
Whitaker, ————	.. ..	Discharged June 10, 1862.
Wardlaw, A. J.	..	

Watson, W. H. .... | July 9. | Discharged September 10, 1862.
Yancy, W. L. .... | March 18. | Absent without leave December 23, 1862.
Yancy, L. D. .... | March 18. | Absent without leave December 23, 1862.

Total number enrolled, 172. Killed, 14; wounded, 10.

COMPANY C.

Name.	Rank.	Date of Enlistment.	Remarks.
J. G. Ballentyne	Captain.	June 6, 1861	Afterward Lieutenant-colonel, Ballentyne's Battalion.
S. P. Bassett	Captain.		Wounded at Medon, Tenn., Aug. 31, 1862, and captured.
John T. Lawler	Captain.		Wounded at Medon August 31, 1862. Wounded at Britton's Lane September 1, 1862. Wounded at Coltiersville Oct. 11, 1863, and soon afterward captured.
W. B. Maxwell	Lieutenant.		Promoted for gallantry. Captured at Lamar, Miss., November 8, 1862. Wounded at Columbia, Tenn., November 25, 1864.
W. B. Winston	Lieutenant.		
Kenneth Garrett	Lieutenant.		Killed at Medon August 31, 1862.
L. B. Higgins	Lieutenant.		
John Albright	Lieutenant.		Absent, sick, October 5, 1864. Wounded at Harrisburg July 14, 1864.
John Colby	Lieutenant.		
Martin S. Armstrong	Lieutenant.		Promoted January 9, 1864.
A. L. Winston	3d Lt.		Wounded at Brice's Cross Roads June 10, 1862, and promoted to Adjutant for gallantry.
John D. Huhn	Sergeant.		
A. Hicks	Sergeant.		
W. D. Nicholson	Sergeant.		
T. J. Lewellen	Sergeant.		

Name.	Rank.	Date of Enlistment.	Remarks.
James Abernathy	Sergeant.	June 6, 1861	Captured February 20, 1863, near Cockrun, Miss
William Griffin	Sergeant.		
D. McCallum	Sergeant.		
Thomas Brocchus	Corporal.	June 6, 1861	Absent without leave May 4, 1864. Mentioned by Gen. Jackson for gallantry at Corinth Oct. 3–5, 1862.
T. J. Lewellen	Corporal.	June 6, 1861	Absent on sick leave October 30, 1862.

Privates.

Name.	Date of Enlistment.	Remarks.
Baugh, John		
Barton, G. W.	Oct. 3, 1861	Absent without leave April 28, 1864.
Briscoe, John		
Butler, W. R.		
Burns, C.	Oct. 1, 1861	Absent without leave October 5, 1862.
Barrett, ——		
Burke, ——		
Bradley, James		
Bullock, James		
Coulton, W.	Sept. 15, 1861	Died January 7, 1864, near Irby Mills, Miss
Campbell, W. R.	Mar. 10, 1862	Absent without leave March 31, 1864.
Calhoun, E. H.	June 6, 1861	Captured at Chulahoma, Miss., October 19, 1863. Absent without leave October 24, 1863.
Card, John	Aug. 6, 1861	Absent without leave February 25, 1864.
Champion, J. T.	Oct. 3, 1861	Killed at Harrisburg July 14, 1864.
Colby, John	July 1, 1861	Afterward Third Lieutenant. Wounded at Harrisburg.
Chambers, Dr		

Carter, Ed James		Killed at Medon August 31, 1862.
Crouch, J. W.	July —, 1861	Absent, sick, October 30, 1862.
Cloud, —		
Curlin, Tom		
Curlin, Zack		
Davidson, T. J.	Feb. 10, 1863	Wounded at Colliersville October 11, 1863. Absent, sick at hospital, February 29, 1864.
Dickey, W. F.	Feb. 16, 1863	Seriously wounded and captured at Colliersville October 11, 1863.
Dekany, —		
Dennis, John		
Davidson, Thomas		
Dickey, John		Killed at Colliersville October 11, 1863.
Dennis, John	June 6, 1861	Absent without leave September 24, 1862.
Edwards, George M.		
Edward, B		
Farris, N. J.		
Farris, W H.	June 6, 1861	Absent without leave April 15, 1864. Captured at Medon, Tenn., September 1, 1862.
Foster, Dr.		
France, —		
Grooms, R.	June 6, 1861	Absent without leave June 18, 1863.
Giridin, E. D.	June 6, 1861	Absent, sick, July 25, 1862. Detailed for duty on general provost guard April 30, 1864.
Gwynne, A		
Gaylor, Ed.		Wounded at Belmont, Mo., 1861.
Grogan, John		Wounded near Columbus, Ky., October 1861; wounded near Holly Springs, Miss., 1863.
Guthrie, —		
Golden, T.		
Golden, M.		

Name.	Date of Enlistment.	Remarks.
Gallager, John		Killed near Paducah, Ky., 1861.
Gwyn, W		Killed at Ripley, Miss., February, 1864.
Hawkins, B. F	Jan. 3, 1864	Sick in hospital at Oxford February 5, 1864.
Hennessy, W		Killed near Nashville December 1, 1864.
Holloway, John M. B.	June 6, 1861	Wounded near Columbus, Ky., October, 1861. Put under arrest May 1, 1864, for insubordination and disobedience of orders.
Hutchison, Benjamin	Aug. 24, 1861	Absent without leave May 9, 1864.
Hyatt, John E		Killed at Harrisburg July 14, 1864.
Hicks, Robert		
Holt, Benjamin		Wounded near Columbus, Ky., October, 1861.
Hickey, William		Killed at Collierville, Tenn., October 11, 1862.
Hillern, J		
Hicks, Alfred		Wounded at Mathews's Ferry, Miss., 1863.
Hoag, William		Wounded at Corinth October 3, 1862.
Hyatt, Thomas		
Hildebrand, Thomas		
Hahn, John D	June 6, 1861	Absent, sick, October 30, 1862. Promoted from Third Sergeant January 9, 1864, to First Sergeant.
Hicks, Robert	Feb. 1, 1863	Dropped from the roll July 18, 1863. Returned February 3, 1864.
Huboa, Joseph	June 6, 1861	Absent at Oxford hospital February 5, 1864.
Keeloe, Joseph		
Kerk, Alexander	June 6, 1861	Absent without leave Oct. 19, 1862. Ambulance corps April 30, 1864.
Kelton, F		
Kindle, William	March 27	Absent without leave May 7, 1864.
Keenan,		
Kerd, John		
Kney, Charles		
Layton, A		

Name	Date	Remarks
Lucas, ——.		
Marr, Thomas.	August 26, ——	Absent without leave April 30, 1864.
Marlow, William.		
Martin, J. M.		
Marks, Samuel.	June 6, 1861	Absent, sick, October 30, 1862, and February 19, 1864.
Mills, J. R.	Sept. 2, 1861	On detached duty October 30, 1862. Absent without leave February 25, 1864.
Miller, Robert.		
Moody, Tillman.	June 6, 1861	Died in Camp Ripley, Tenn., 1862.
Murrah, J. K.		
Moseley, George.	Sept. 25, 1861	January 30, 1864, detached to Medical Department.
Maccabe, J. C.		Died in camp in Panola, Miss.
McFadden, ——.		Wounded at Brice's Cross Roads June 10, 1864.
Murray, James.		
May, Richard.		
McMahan, ——.		
Mullin, ——.		
Moyston, W.	Oct. 25, 1861	Absent without leave September 5, 1862, and April 28, 1864.
Norwood, John P.	May 1, 1861	Wounded at Medon August 31, 1862.
Norvell, Stal.		
Norman, Thomas.		
Nicholas, W.		
Owen, Lemuel.	July 1, 1863	Shot by horse thieves February 19, 1864.
O'Neill, I.		
Parker, Samuel B.		
Parks, D. J.		
Paul, Willis.		
Poag, Thomas.	Sept. 15, 1861	Absent without leave May 30, 1864.
Pruden, J. R.		
Pugh, W.		

Name.	Date of Enlistment.	Remarks.
Parks, G.		
Pruden, L.		
Phelan, Joseph.		
Palmer, W.		
Ridgeway, A. D.		
Reach, C. T.	July 7, 1861	Absent without leave March 11, 1864. Died in 1864, in Shelby County, Tenn.
Roff, John W.	Jan. 20, 1863	Absent without leave January 25, 1864.
Scott, George.		
Stevens, P. H.		Killed at Harrisburg July 14, 1864.
Stoveall, ——		
Sarrens, John.		
Somers, W.	Aug. 1, 1862	Sick near Hernando October, 1862.
Sutherland, John.		
Stephenson, John.		Severely wounded at Britton's Lane or Medon.
Stevens, J.	May 15, 1861	Captured at Medon September 1, 1862.
Thelan, Joseph.	June 6, 1861	Wounded October 3; at Corinth, Miss. Absent without leave January 2, 1864.
Thompson, O. M.		Killed near Hernando, Miss., 1862.
Tate, G.		
Volner, Frederick.	May 15, 1861	Detached as gunsmith, at Oxford, March 7, 1863.
Wells, William.	Feb. 1, 1864	Absent without leave April 30, 1864.
Wright, George.		
Woodlock, H. P.		
Ward, A. J.		
Wilds, W.		
Wright, W.		
Witt, J.		

Winston, Arthur........July 19, 1862 { Promoted from First Sergeant January 9, 1864. Absent, sick, January 19, 1864, to April 30, 1864; resignation forwarded; awaiting action on sick leave; died in service.

Wilds, F.......... ┐
Wright, C.......... ┘

NOTE.—No information could be obtained concerning this company except the roster which is given below. The company was disbanded in May, 1862, most of the members joining other companies in the same regiment.

COMPANY D (WHITE'S).

Roll of Officers.

Captain, White, J. S.
Lieutenant, Stocks, W. T.
Lieutenant, Hall, William.
Lieutenant, Montgomery, William.
Lieutenant, Moore, A. R.
Orderly Sergeant, McKnight, James

Members and Non-commissioned Officers.

Armour, William D.	Brinkley, Stephen,	Dixon, Henry
Ayers, Thomas	Baud, Samuel	Bashiell, E. H.
Albertson, John	Berthold, William	Davis, Samuel
Black, B. Sc.	Christian, Walter	Dennis, Benjamin
Baker, Charles	Conry, John	Forrest, N. B.
Balis, William	Champ, Jack	Forrest, William
Bradley, Joe	Coulter, R. B.	Forrest, Jeffrey
Birmingham, Greene	Cornelius, John	Fowler, A. S.
Boyd, Thomas	Campbell, Jack	Fentress, John
Browning, A. J.	Coupwood, W. J.	Finch, John

Fields, John
Gallagher, Hugh
Goeh, Jack
Gilbert, J.
Humphries, Jack
Hains, Ross
Hilderbrand, John
Hart, Samuel
Hessing, Charles
Healing, John

174 *The Seventh Tennessee Cavalry.*

Members and Non-commissioned Officers (Continued).

Harper, Joe	Miller, R. B.	Purcell, Barney	Stout, Sam
Jackson, A.	Miller, R. R.	Parks, Densy	Snow, H.
Jones, William	McClure, Paggy	Porter, Albert	Tandy, James
Klinger, John	Moore, William	Priston, Christopher	Tilford, R. H.
Klink, Clinton	Mahan, Peter	Priestor, John	Tuff, Harry
Louden, James	Mosley, Sam	Pattie, J. R.	Thomas, Jack
Layton, Abe	Myers, Gus	Robson, B. P.	Vouzn, C. H.
Laundry, Dryel	Mageveny, Hugh	Rulman, William J.	Valmer, Fritz
Luxton, Joe	McMahon, James	Richmond, Barton	Ward, A. J.
McMurry, James	McClaughlin, James	Stephens, Jack	Wells, James
Montgomery, Ed	Norvil, Sam	Smith, Jackson	Winters, Thomas
Montgomery, William	Pleasants, Brooks	Sanderson, Robert	

Company D.

Name.	Rank.	Date of Enlistment.	Remarks.
R. W Haywood.	Captain.		Elected Captain May 22, 1862. Wounded and captured at Lamar, Miss., November 8, 1862.
L. W Taliaferro.	Captain.	May 15, 1861	Resigned.
L. H. Johnson...	Lieutenant.		Wounded at Bolivar August 30, 1862. Afterward Colonel Seventh Tennessee.
W L. Duckworth.	Lieutenant.		Resigned.
J. W Jones.....	Lieutenant.		Resigned.
J. M. Shaw.....	Lieutenant.		Elected First Lieutenant May 22, 1862. Wounded at Columbia, Tenn, November 25, 1864.
H. J. Livingston.	Lieutenant.	May 23, 1861	

Name		Remarks
James Bond	Lieutenant.	
T. B. Mann	Lieutenant.	
A. A. Johnson	Lieutenant.	Wounded at Spring Hill, Tenn., November 29, 1864.
J. H. Reid	Lieutenant.	Wounded at Medon August 31, 1861. Resigned September, 1863.
J. Eader	Sergeant.	Appointed First Sergeant May 1, 1862. Captured twice during the war.
H. G. Winfield	Sergeant. May 23, 1861	Appointed Second Sergeant June 15, 1862.
M. McGrath	Sergeant. May 23, 1861	Appointed Third Sergeant January 11, 1862.
J. C. Halloway	Sergeant. May 23, 1861	Appointed Fourth Sergeant June 15, 1862. Captured March 3, 1864. Died in prison at Camp Douglass.
R. W. Grizzard	Sergeant.	
W. C. George	Sergeant. May 23, 1861	Appointed Fifth Sergeant June 15, 1862.
J. L. Elwood	Corporal. Aug. 17, 1861	Appointed Third Corporal June 15, 1862. Killed at Columbia, Tenn., November 25, 1864.
E. D. Dupree	Corporal. May 23, 1861	Absent without leave April 15, 1864.
R. S. Erwin	Corporal.	
D. Dodge	Corporal.	
S. W. Calvin	Corporal. May 23, 1861	On furlough April 20, 1864. Captured twice during war.
R. V Mann	Corporal. May 23, 1861	Appointed First Corporal June 15, 1862. Absent without leave October 30, 1862.
T. R. Claiborne	Corporal. June 1, 1861	Appointed Second Corporal June 15, 1862. Appointed Fourth Corporal June 15, 1862.

Privates.

Name	Date of Enlistment.	Remarks.
Anthony, W. L.	May 23, 1861	Wounded at Medon August 31, 1862.
Austin, A. S		Discharged June, 1861, to command militia as Colonel.
Archer, P. C.	May 23, 1861	Detailed with sharp-shooters October 30, 1862; and Medical Department May 11, 1864. Wounded at Collierville October 11, 1863.

Name.	Date of Enlistment.	Remarks.
Austin, Edward		
Austin, A. M.		
Almand, C. E.		Discharged May, 1862, on reorganization.
Anderson, H. C.		
Allison, J. F.	May 23, 1861	Absent on surgeon's certificate October 30, 1862. Discharged sick July 20, 1863.
Aldridge, S. H.		Discharged May, 1862, at reorganization.
Blair, S. J.	July 4, 1861	Absent without leave October 30, 1862.
Barber, J. F.		Captured November 8, 1862; December 3, 1862.
Becker, William		
Bond, Lewis		
Browning, R. H.	Oct. 1, 1861	Promoted to Lieutenant of Artillery in the fall of 1861. Wounded at Medon August 31, 1862.
Baker, W. T.		
Blake, W. A.		
Benson, G. W.	June 11, 1861	Appointed Bugler for Gen. W. H. Jackson May 24, 1862, and discharged.
Bradford, W. A.	Aug. 28, 1863	Detailed as teamster January, 1864, by order of Col. Duckworth.
Boyd, Allison	July 1, 1863	Absent without leave October 30, 1862.
Bond, W. P., Jr.		
Bradford, Miles H.		
Benson, Gil.	May 23, 1861	Absent without leave October 30, 1862.
Claiborne, T. B. L.		Mortally wounded and captured at Old Lamar, Miss., November 8, 1862; and died of wounds at La Grange November 11, 1862.
Cole, S. W.	May 23, 1861	Absent without leave June, 1862.
Chapman, B. W.	May 23, 1861	Absent without leave April 15, 1864.
Calvin, Z.		
Curry, W. S.	Aug. 6, 1862	Absent, sick, October 30, 1862; and without leave May 1, 1864.
Cole, John D.		Discharged June, 1861, to take command of militia as Brigadier-general.

Colton, ——		
Day, Frank		Sick at Panola, Miss., August 16, 1863.
Davie, B. P.		
Davis, T. A.		Discharged sick in the winter of 1861–62.
Dupree, E. D.	May 23, 1861	Second Corporal. Absent without leave April 15, 1864.
Davis, J. W	May 23, 1861	Discharged as over age under Conscript Act, reorganization May 23, 1862.
Estes, A. M.		Wounded at Spring Hill November 29, 1864.
Estes, T. H.		
Epperson, J. L.	May 23, 1861	Absent on furlough October 30, 1862.
Estes, J. H.		
Elder, Charles		Promoted Lieutenant Aide-de-camp by Gen. W. Y. C. Hunes, 1863.
Estes, C. A.		
Elder, James		Wounded at Brice's Cross Roads June 10, 1862.
Evans, J. T.		
Elwood, J. L.		Killed at Harrisburg, Miss., July 14, 1864.
Edwards, B. T		
Freeman, John H	June 20, 1862	Absent, sick, May 25, 1864.
Freeman, J. Hart.		Wounded at Franklin, November 30, 1864.
Frink, M. M.	July 20, 1861	Captured at Melon August 31, 1862.
Freeman, Hardy.		
Furgeson, Milton.		Discharged sick.
Grove, E. S.	May 23, 1861	Third Corporal. Mortally wounded at Melon, Tenn., August 31, 1862. Died September 1, 1862.
George, W. C.	May 23, 1861	Died in camp, 1863.
Griffin, B. F.	May 23, 1861	Absent without leave April 30, 1864.
Griffin, J. B.	May 23, 1861	May 11, 1864, detailed to Forage Department, order Col. Duckworth.
Garrison, J. L.		
Grizard, W. H. L.	May 23,	Absent without leave from October 23, 1862. Rejoined the regiment April 25, 1864, and killed at Harrisburg July 14, 1864.

Name.	Date of Enlistment.	Remarks.
Grove, R. R.		Captured at Medon August 31, 1862. Transferred to Company L, 1863.
Garrison, T. B.	May 23, 1861	Absent without leave June 1, 1862.
Green, S. P.	July 10, 1861	Absent without leave July 4, 1862.
Holloway, John C.		Died in prison, 1853.
Hawkins, J. J		
Harbert, B. F		Discharged at reorganization, May, 1862.
Hassell, William	Aug. 4, 1862	February 29, 1864, absent wounded since March, 1862.
Henderson, Eli.	May 23, 1861	In hospital at Grenada, Miss., October 30, 1862.
Henly, Thomas		
Henly, Theophilus G.	May 23, 1861	Absent without leave June 1, 1862.
Hawkins, J. B.	May 23, 1861	Absent without leave June 1, 1862.
Halliburton, J. W	June 24, 1861	Absent without leave June 6, 1862.
Hodge, R. R	May 23, 1861	Absent without leave June 15, 1862.
Irvine, Dr. Alex.	Aug. 1, 1861	Absent, sick in Haywood County, Tenn., April 1, 1864.
Irvine, R. S		
Jarrett, Henry.	May 23, 1861	Killed at Rutlidge's farm, near Okolona, February 22, 1864.
Jeffries, Robert.		
Jones, Buck.		
Kee, Joseph.		Discharged, over age, May 23, 1862.
Koonce, J. T.		
Keller		From the United States regular army.
Livingston, T. C	May 23, 1861	Absent on sick leave April 25, 1864.
Lowe, J. B.		
Legett, Noah.	May 23, 1861	Wounded at Medon August 31, 1862.
Lucas, J. H		
Lucas, J.	May 7, 1864	Joined by transfer May 7, 1864.
Lilly, John S.	May 23, 1861	Blacksmith. Absent without leave June 3, 1862.

McGee, W. C.		Killed at Collierville, Tenn., October 11, 1863.
Mann, R.		
Mann, Joel.		
Mann, R. V		
Miller		
Mehane, E. G.		
Moore, John	May 23, 1861	Wounded at Harrisburg August 14, 1864.
Morton, J. H.	May 23, 1861	Discharged, over age, May 23, 1862.
Northcross, J. W.		
Northcross, Thomas	May 23, 1861	Killed at Yockana Bridge, Miss., 1863.
Nolen, H. C.	May 23, 1861	Absent without leave June 1, 1862.
Owen, Ed.		Killed at Harrisburg July 14, 1864.
Oldham, R. F		
Owen, W. C.	May 23, 1861	Discharged May 23, 1862.
Penn, H. L.		
Perkins, T. M.		
Parker, J. P	Sept. 28, 1861	At hospital in Grenada, Miss., October 30, 1862.
Porter, R. S.	May 23, 1861	Absent without leave June 1, 1862.
Perry, Thomas	Nov. 25, 1861	Absent, surgeon's certificate, October 30, 1862.
Patterson, J. B.	July 4, 1861	Detailed with sharp-shooters October 30, 1862.
Raines, H.	Oct. 22, 1862	Absent without leave April 25, 1864.
Raines, R. F., Jr.		
Robinson, M. W	May 27, 1861	Absent, sick certificate, October 30, 1862.
Rhodes, G. J		
Read, A. T.		Discharged at reorganization, May, 1862.
Rhodes, R. H.		
Robinson, Rom.		Killed near Fort Pemberton, Miss., March 27, 1868.
Robinson, J. F.		
Shirley, B.		Died December 27, 1861.
Saunders, J. W.	Dec. 20, 1861	Wounded and captured at Medon, August 31, 1862, and discharged.

Name.	Date of Enlistment.	Remarks.
Smith, J. H.	June 10, 1861	Absent without leave June 1, 1862.
Smith, W H.	Apr. 25, 1864	Transferred to Fifteenth Tennessee Cavalry May 7, 1864.
Shore Alle.		Shot accidentally at Jackson, Tenn., and discharged.
Sallis, W H.	May 23, 1861	Captured and paroled by the enemy October, 1862. February 29, 1864, absent without leave.
Strickland, P. H.		
Schawb, W. H.	May 2, 1861	Bugler. Absent without leave May 1, 1862.
Scrope, Joseph		
Smith, T. G.	?	Killed near Eaton, Tenn., 1862.
Shaw, Sol.		
Scrope, Alexander		
Swetland, E.	May 23, 1861	Discharged under conscript act May 23, 1862.
Smith, G. T.	Apr. 25, 1864	Transferred to Fifteenth Tennessee Cavalry May 7, 1864.
Tucker, William W.		Wounded at Medon August 31, 1862.
Taliaferro, E. D.		Transferred to Company L, 1863.
Taliaferro, B. D.		
Tharpe, J.		Wounded at Harrisburg July 14, 1864.
Tyler, T. B.	May 23, 1861	Absent without leave June 1, 1862.
Taylor, F. M.		Discharged at Camp Beauregard in the fall of 1861.
Wright, James		
Walker, L. G.		Rejoined April 17, 1864.
Whitehurst, B. A.		
Wilson, Paca.		
Whitelaw, W M.		Promoted to Lieutenant infantry, and discharged 1861.
Weaver, M.		
Wells, John S.	May 23, 1861	Absent without leave October 30, 1862.
Weaver, E.	May 23, 1861	Absent without leave October 30, 1862.

Colored Men with Company.

Dupree, Warner	Livingston, Essex	Mann, Frank	Allison, March
Anthony, Benjamin	Barber, Henry	Bond, Warrick	Demoss, Claiborne
Doris, Prince	Irwin, Albert (Major Mud)	Tucker, Ed	Freeman, Joseph
Robinson, Mose	Johnson, Chapman	Mann, Thomas	Walker, Dick
Jarrett, Thompson	Reed, Alexander	Taylor, Cornelius	Perkins, John
Taylor, Aaron	Wilson, John	Northcross, Henry	Haliburton, Anthony

COMPANY E.

Name.	Rank.	Date of Enlistment.	Remarks.
J. J. Neely	Captain.		
W. J. Tate	Captain.	May 24, 1861	Wounded, June 9, 1863, at ——. Killed near Ripley, Miss., June 11, 1864.
J. P. Statler	Captain.	May 24, 1861	Wounded February 22, 1864, at Prairie Mound. Killed at Harrisburg July 14, 1864.
T. P. Harris	Lieutenant.		Died in service.
F. G. Patrick	Lieutenant.		
Leon Bills	Lieutenant.		
W. W. McCauley	Lieutenant.		
H. Harris	Lieutenant.		
W. C. Mashburn	Lieutenant.		Killed at Athens, Ala, September, 1864.
V. S. Ruffin	Lieutenant.		Died in service at Abbeville, Miss.
Fisk Weaver	Lieutenant.	May 23, 1861	Absent without leave September 10, 1862.
T. W. Crawford	1st Serg.		
J. W. Nelson	2d Serg.		
A. M. Statler			

Name.	Rank.	Date of Enlistment.	Remarks.
R. D. Durrett	3d Serg.	May 24, 1861	Detailed commanding scout in Tennessee May 11, 1864.
F. Fentress	4th Serg.		
W. C. Hardy	5th Serg.		
J. V. Field	1st Corp.		
Hardy Mashburn	2d Corp.	Mar. 11, 1863	Sick, furlough, March 11, 1863.
C. B. Linthicum	3d Corp.	Sept. 15, 1861	Detached as scout for General Buford, May 11, 1864.

Privates.

Name.	Date of Enlistment.	Remarks.
Allen, John F		Killed at Britton's Lane September 1, 1862.
Allen, John	May 24, 1861	Wounded, and left in Tennessee, May 2, 1864.
Berry, B		
Bradford, J. W		Killed at Britton's Lane September 1, 1862.
Bradford, G		
Brown, F. N	May 24, 1861	Left with wounded February 22, 1864, at Prairie Mound.
Brown, R. N		
Blaylock, E. P	May 24, 1861	Left with wounded February 22, 1864, at Prairie Mound.
Benson, W. L	May 24, 1861	Under arrest at Panola February 29, 1864. Rejoined April 4, 1864.
Brewer, Samuel		
Burford, J. D		
Billington, R. L	Dec. 11, 1861	Left sick on march February 21, 1864.
Bright, G. P		
Breden, William		
Brewer, J. H		
Barrett, John		

Burkhead, E.		
Barnett, P. M	Mar. 11, 1863	Absent with leave January 11, 1864. Ordered dropped from company roll April 4, 1864. Rejoined.
Boucher, T. P.		Killed at Brice's Cross Roads June 10, 1864.
Blaylock, Stanton		Wounded.
Breeland, John	Mar. 16, 1863	Killed at Britton's Lane September 1, 1862.
Baker, James	Mar. 11, 1863	Rejoined April 15, 1864.
Baker, L. K.	Mar. 11, 1863	Rejoined April 15, 1864.
Baker, George	Mar. 11, 1863	Rejoined April 15, 1864.
Crow, Charles		
Carraway, J. E.		Wounded at Britton's Lane September 1, 1862.
Cross, N. B.	May 24, 1861	Wounded at Britton's Lane September 1, 1862; detailed as bugler February 1, 1864.
Cansby, F.		
Carruth, W. H.	May 24, 1861	Detailed as blacksmith April 14, 1863.
Campbell, George		
Clinton, S. H.	May 24, 1861	Absent, wounded, since October 11, 1863 (at Collierville).
Cheshire, James	June 2, 1863	Absent without leave, May 2, 1864.
Cheshire, John	Mar. 15, 1863	Rejoined April 15, 1864. Absent without leave May 2, 1864.
Curry, J. W.	Feb. 1, 1862	Detailed on duty in Tennessee May 11, 1864.
Campbell, William H.		
Crawford, Thomas		
Curry, William		
Chalmers, J. H.	Sept. 11, 1863	Absent without leave April 4, 1864.
Cheshire, H.		
Cheshire, W.		
Connelly, J. D.	May 24, 1861	Wounded at Britton's Lane September 1, 1862.
Campbell, W. T.	May 24, 1861	Rejoined March 15, 1864.
Davis, J.		
Dougherty, J.	May 24, 1861	

Name.	Date of Enlistment.	Remarks.
Barrett, R.		On duty in Tennessee May 11, 1864.
Barrett, D. E.	May 24, 1861	Killed at Harrisburg July 14, 1864.
Bonegan, F.		Wounded at Britton's Lane September 1, 1862.
Dunlap, J. F.	May 24, 1861	
David, J. B.		On duty in Tennessee May 11, 1864.
Duncan, J. W.		
Davis, M.		Wounded at Prairie Mound February 22, 1864.
Durrett, J. W.	May 24, 1861	Killed accidentally in service.
Denham, A. H.	June 7, 1863	Detailed by Col. Jackson October 16, 1862.
Erwin, Joseph	Mar. 11, 1863	Detailed as scout in Tennessee May 3, 1864.
Field, J. V.		Rejoined April 17, 1864.
Fentress, James	May 15, 1861	Killed at Harrisburg July 14, 1864.
Fortune, R. L.	May 11, 1861	Absent on surgeon's certificate February 29, 1864; certificate of permanent disability May 11, 1864.
Ferrit, William		
Fortune, J. T.	Aug. 5, 1861	Wounded at Britton's Lane September 1, 1862.
Foppiano, John		
Fulcham, William		
Fossain, John	Dec. 19, 1861	Captured October 1, 1862, at Pocahontas. Died in service, Grenada, Miss., February, 1863.
Foster, A. John		
Fulton, ——	May 24, 1861	Rejoined April 4, 1864.
Ferrill, W. B.		
Gilchrist, A.		
Gillespie, J. W.		
Gordon, William		
Gillespie, Thomas	Aug. 25, 1862	Detailed on duty in Tennessee May 11, 1864.
Gibson, Wm. (Sam?)		Killed at Harrisburg July 14, 1864.
Grove, J. H.		

Name	Date	Remarks
Gibson, Jesse	May 24, 1861	On special duty October 30, 1862.
Harris, E. A.	Apr. 15, 1863	Absent with leave February 29, 1863. May 11, 1864, transferred to Twelfth Tennessee Cavalry.
Hubbard, J. M.	May 24, 1861	Absent with leave May 11, 1864.
Harris, Orris		Absent with leave May 11, 1864.
Higgs, Wiley	May 24, 1861	Detailed at Coldwater by Col. Jackson October, 1862.
Harris, H.	May 24, 1864	Horse killed March 2, 1864, at Bolivar.
Hartigan, M.		Wounded at Britton's Lane September 1, 1862.
Harris, G. F., Dr.		
Harrison, C. L.	May 24, 1861	Detailed as Commissary Sergeant March 1, 1863.
Hundly, James		
Hornsby, Willie		
Hornsby, Mat.		
Hackney, James		
Harris, E. A.		
Hughes, N. E.		Killed at Tishomingo Creek June 10, 1864.
Hardy, William		Wounded at Britton's Lane September 1, 1862, after R.
Hardrye, Morris		
Henline, H.		
Hillhouse, N		
Hill, Jerome		Discharged.
Hays, S.		
Jones, Lem		
Jackson, F. M.		
Jones, Jack		
Joyner, J. F.	May 24, 1861	
Joyner, J. Thomas	May 24, 1861	Wounded at Britton's Lane September 1, 1862.
Johnson, Zeno		
Kirkland, Joseph		
Lambert, John		

Name.	Date of Enlistment.	Remarks.
Lambert, Robert		
Lawton, A. H.		
Lackey, L. J.		
Lay, May		
Lewis, ——		
McGuire, Thomas.		
Moore, J. A.		
McKinnie, William.	Mar. 11, 1863	{ Detailed as blacksmith April 14, 1863. Killed at Harrisburg July 14, 1864.
McKinnie, David.	Mar. 11, 1863	{ Detailed as scout May 3, 1864, by order of Gen. Forrest. Killed at Harrisburg, Miss., July 14, 1864.
McKinnie, P. H.	Mar. 11, 1863	Wounded, and left in Tennessee, May 2, 1864.
McKinnie, M. J		Rejoined January 20, 1864. Absent without leave May 2, 1864.
Mashburn, B. F		
Mays, Dr.		
Myrick, W. F.	Sept. 29, 1863	Detailed as scout May 3, 1864.
Moore, James		Killed in battle.
Marr, Joseph		Killed in battle.
Nelson, W. R	May 24, 1861	Detailed to drive ambulance November 1, 1862.
Nelson, J. W., Sr		
Neel, R. K.		
Nichols, William.		
Neely, C. R.		Killed at Harrisburg (or Brice's Cross Roads) July 14, 1864.
Nuckles, William.		
Nuckles, William, Jr.		
Noment, E. L.		{ Absent without leave February 1, 1864. Killed in personal difficulty, at Jackson, April 29, 1864.
Neel, Joseph		

Neil (Clint), G. C.	May 24, 1861	Rejoined April 15, 1864.
Phillips, S.	Mar. 11, 1863	Wounded, and left in Tennessee, April 11, 1864.
Phillips, Solomon	Mar. 11, 1863	Absent with leave January 11, 1864; ordered dropped from roll.
Polk, W. A.		
Piles, James	May 24, 1861	Rejoined April 12, 1864.
Perkins, A. H. D.		Promoted Color Sergeant, May 18, 1864, for gallantry on field. Wounded at Colliersville, Brice's Cross Roads, Okolona, and Franklin.
Piles, S.		
Phillips, N. P.	Mar. 11, 1863	Absent without leave February 15, 1864. Rejoined April 4, 1864. Absent without leave May 2, 1864.
Price, J. W.	Mar. 11, 1863	Absent without leave February 15, 1864. Rejoined April 12, 1864.
Pipkins, Steven		
Pipkin, J. H.		Killed at Brice's Cross Roads June 10, 1864.
Pipkin, David		
Perth, George		
Pipkin, Samuel	Oct. 9, 1861	Rejoined January 28, 1864. Died near Aberdeen April 5, 1864, of fever.
Pertle, G.	May 24, 1861	Rejoined January 20, 1864; absent without leave May 2, 1864.
Ruffin, T.		
Ruffin, J.		
Rainey, James		
Sawyer, J. T.		Wounded at Medon or Britton's Lane.
Sturtivant, J. T.		
Spurlock, W. J.	May 24, 1861	Absent without leave May 1, 1864.
Sullivan, Tim		Accidentally drowned.
Statler, O.		
Scott, William		
Schroggins, J.		
Tierney, Thomas	May 24, 1861	Detailed as scout May 3, 1864.

Name.	Date of Enlistment.	Remarks.
Thompson, L		
Tatum, R. G.	May 24, 1861	Detailed as farrier September 1, 1863.
Tate, N	May 24, 1861	Detailed at Grenada in ———, 1882.
Tatum, P. B.	May 24, 1861	Detailed to Assistant Quartermaster's Department September 1, 1863.
Tisdale, L. W	May 24, 1861	Rejoined January 20, 1864. Absent without leave May 1, 1864.
Terry, Eli	Mar. 11, 1863	Absent with leave May 11, 1864.
Taylor, W. A.		
Upton, T. R.	May 24, 1861	Absent without leave October, 1862.
Wood, John		
Weatherly, J. H.		
Wood, P. D.		
Wood, William		Killed at Harrisburg July 14, 1864.
Wood, Samuel		
Webb, M. D.	May 24, 1861	Left sick in Tennessee, May 1, 1864.
Webb, J. R.	May 24, 1861	Absent, wounded at Okolona, February 22, 1864.
Wenders, Willie		Killed at Britton's Lane September 1, 1862.

COMPANY F.

Name.	Rank.	Date of Enlistment.	Remarks.
C. C. Clay	Captain.	Nov. 4, 1861	Afterward Major of Seventh Tennessee. Wounded at Prairie Mound February 22, 1864. Wounded at Harrisburg July 14, 1864.
C. H. Jones	Captain.		
H. G. Winburne	Lieutenant.		
J. E. Gregory	Lieutenant.		
W. W Robertson	Lieutenant.		Killed at Brice's Cross Roads June 10, 1864.

Name		Date of Enlistment	Remarks
J. A. Everett	1st Sergt.		Killed at Columbia, Tenn., November 25, 1864.
G. W. Richard	2d Sergt.		Absent, sick, February 29, 1864.
James Sinclair	3d Sergt.		
J. M. Baker	4th Sergt.		

Privates.

Name	Date of Enlistment	Remarks
Allen, J.		
Aiken, William L.	May 4, 1864	Discharged October 20, 1862.
Ashley, H. C.		Absent without leave October 30, 1862.
Bradley, Joe	Nov. 4, 1861	Rejoined April 18, 1864.
Barrett, M.		
Bell, John		
Bell, Ransom		
Baker, Joe		
Bridges, John H.	Nov. 4, 1861	Rejoined April, 1864.
Barnett, William		Detailed to wait on wounded October 30, 1862.
Casey, B.	Apr. 18, 1864	Absent without leave May 6, 1864.
Costillo, T. J.		
Casey, J. C.	Nov. 4, 1861	Rejoined April 18, 1864.
Caton, Alexander	May 22, 1861	Captured near Vicksburg December 26, 1863.
Chilicutt, A.	Nov. 10, 1861	Discharged May 20, 1862.
Cousins, R.		
Daniel, Thomas		
Duffy, Henry		
Davis, Tom		
Evans, T. F.		
Everett, L.	Aug. 20, 1865	Absent, sick, with leave August 20, 1861.

Name.	Date of Enlistment.	Remarks.
Ellington, D.		
English, V		
English, Q.		
Fleetwood, G. B	Nov. 4, 1861	Rejoined April, 1864. Absent without leave May 6, 1864.
Freeno, James R.	April, 1862.	Transferred to Capt. J. A. Taylor's Company September 30, 1862.
Faulkner, Henry	Nov. 4, 1861	Rejoined April 18, 1864.
Fox, Harry	Nov. 4, 1861	Discharged October 29, 1862.
Guthrie, Henry.		
Guthrie, J. T		
Haynes, T. J		
Howell, Jake.	Nov. 4, 1861	Detailed as teamster October 30, 1862.
Houston, W. S.	Mch. 13, 1862	Absent without leave March 13, 1864. Wounded.
Hedley, J. H.		
Howard, Charles.		
Hugins, H.	Nov. 4, 1861	Discharged March 15, 1862.
Hughes, A.		
Hughes, James	March, 1862.	Wounded at Ripley, Miss, October 7, 1862.
Hathaway, D. A.	Nov. 4, 1861	Absent without leave October 30, 1862.
Jenkins, J. W		Killed in battle.
Jewell, Ennice	Apr. 18, 1864	Absent without leave May 8, 1854.
Johnson, J. E. F.	Apr. 18, 1864	Absent without leave May 1, 1864.
Jenkins, Samuel.		
Key, L. C.		Transferred to Company L August 27, 1862.
Klyce, Mat.	Nov. 4, 1861	Absent without leave October 30, 1862.
Lewis, G. B.		
Locke, James.		
Latham, James		
Lynn, W E.		
Lytle, B. J		

Name	Date	Remarks
Marr, J. M.	Sept. 15, 1861	Detailed as scout May, 1864, by order of Col. Duckworth.
Moss, G. W.	Nov. 4, 1861	Detailed as courier to Gen. Villipigue October, 1862.
Marlow, M. H.		
Matthews, George		
McClellan, R. E.		
McIntosh, S. B.		{ Discharged October 28, 1862. Detailed as scout by order of Col. Duckworth May 11, 1864.
McKinnon, N. E.	Nov. 4, 1862	Rejoined April 18, 1864.
Miller, John		
Medlin, M.	Nov. 4, 1861	Rejoined April 18, 1864. Absent without leave May 8, 1864.
Mings, Alex.		
Mitchell, O. W.	Nov. 4, 1861	Rejoined April 18, 1864.
McClannahan, J. R.		
McClelland, R. N.	Nov. 4, 1861	Captured August 30, 1862. Rejoined April 18, 1864.
Mitchell, Buck		
Mathis, Jack	Nov. 4, 1861	Absent, sick, October 30, 1862.
Mathis, James		
Mathis, Bob		
McLemore, Dr. A. M.	Nov. 4, 1861	Died September 30, 1862.
Matthews, J. T.		
Nance, P. B.		Killed at Jackson, Tenn, March, 1864.
Norvell, Jake		
Norment, E. L.	April 18, 1862	Transferred to Company L September, 1862.
Odell, S. K.		Wounded at Brice's Cross Roads.
Pearson, T. J.		
Payne, James		
Pementer, R	Nov. 4, 1861	Rejoined April 18, 1864.
Pitman, John		
Powell, W. A.	Aug. 22, 1861	Detailed as teamster August 24, 1864, by order of Col. Duckworth.
Payne, Thomas C	Nov. 4, 1861	Captured at Ripley on retreat from Corinth October 6, 1862.

Name.	Date of Enlistment.	Remarks.
Pitman, J. H.		
Roach, Owen		
Richards, James	Nov. 4, 1861	Rejoined April 18, 1864.
Richards, William		Bell's Depot. Transferred to "Sharp-shooters" October, 1862.
Richards, A.		
Roberson, J. A.		
Robinson, Samuel		Wounded September 15, 1862.
Roberts, D. E.		
Rosser, W. E.		
Roberts, W W		
Ricks, Ed.		Wounded; lost leg at Humboldt.
Roper, Tom		
Revell, A. C.		
Revell, Hardy N		Transferred to "Sharp-shooters" October, 1862.
Read, J. C.		Detailed as Ordnance Sergeant October, 1862.
Rodman, F. J		Wounded September 15, 1862.
Smith, N. H		Discharged September 30, 1862.
Sorter, T. J.		
Sinclair, James		
Smoch, J C		
Spencer, Joe		
Strickland, C.		Discharged May 10, 1862.
Saunders, Britt.		
Sutton, T		
Sullivan, Tim.		
Smothers, J. C		Transferred to "Sharp-shooters" October, 1862.
Sorter, J. G.		Detailed as mechanic October, 1862.
Sutton, J. B		Captured September 15, 1862.

Name			
Smith, N. H.			Discharged September 29, 1862.
Sullivan, Tim.			
Smothers, J. C.			Transferred to sharpshooters October, 1862.
Sexton, J. G.			Detailed as mechanic October, 1862.
Sutton, J. B.			Captured September 15, 1862.
Tucker, William H			
Tribble, F.			Killed in battle.
Teanson, Ed. T			Transferred to Company I, September, 1862.
Taylor, W. T			Detailed as courier to Gen. Villipigue October, 1862.
Teanson, D. J.			Transferred to Company I, September, 1862.
Tucker, J. P.			Died June 28, 1862.
William, Terrell	Nov. 4, 1861	Rejoined April 18, 1864.	Absent without leave April 30, 1864.
Wade, R. C	Sept. 12, 1861	Captured in Kentucky in April, 1864.
Wallace, J. L.	Sept. 15, 1861	Absent without leave May 11, 1864.
Webb, W. E.	Nov. 1, 1861	Rejoined April 18, 1864.
Williams, W. S.	Mar. 4, 1862	Rejoined April 18, 1864.
Williams, W. P.			
Williams, S. M.			
Weldon, George G.			Died near Brownsville, April 23, 1864.
Witherspoon, Wm.			Transferred to Company I, September, 1862.
Webb, John.			
Witherspoon, H. H.			Transferred to Company I, September, 1862.
Webb, Robert.			
Wortham, Yancy			Captured at Ripley Miss., October, 1862.
Willet, W. D.			Died in prison.
Wright, W.			Died in camp.
Welsh, W.			
Wade, Peter.			
Young, Samuel H.	Nov. 4, 1861	Wounded at Medon, or Britton's Lane, 1862. Rejoined Apr. 18, 1864.

Company G.

Name.	Rank.	Date of Enlistment.	Remarks.
James G. Starks	Captain.	Nov. 13, 1861	Afterward Colonel of Seventh Tennessee Regiment.
F F. Aden	Captain.	Oct. 4, 1861	Promoted to Captain July 1, 1862. Wounded at Brice's Cross Roads June 10, 1864.
John J. Blake	Lieutenant.	Oct. 19, 1861	Promoted to First Lieutenant July 1, 1862. On sick leave April 27, 1864.
Benjamin M. Diggs	Lieutenant.	Oct. 25, 1861	Promoted to Second Lieutenant July 1, 1862. Mortally wounded at Davis's Mills, December 21, 1862.
J. T. Haynes	Lieutenant.		
W. N. Griffin	Lieutenant.	Oct. 4, 1861	Elected Lieutenant August 27, 1862.
W. A. Wright	Sergeant.		
P. J. Diggs	Sergeant.	Oct. 25, 1861	Sick at Starksville February 29, 1864.
T. F Diggs	Sergeant.	Nov. 28, 1861	Absent with leave May 1, 1864.
H. A. Humphreys	Sergeant.	Nov. 20, 1861	Absent, sick, March 20, 1864.
G. I. Cullchouse	Sergeant.	Oct. 12, 1861	Left sick near Mount Tippah July, 1862.
L. P. Atkinson	Corporal.		
J. R. Anderson	Corporal.		
E. T. Looney	Corporal.		
Thomas Diggs	Corporal.		
—— Bishop	Corporal.		
William Courts	Corporal.		
R. S. Vandyck	Corporal.	Nov. 25, 1861	Sick October 6, 1862.
Martin, J. P.	Corporal.		

Privates.

Name.	Date of Enlistment.	Remarks.
Aden, J. D	Sept. 21, 1863	Absent, sick, near Grenada, February 12, 1864. Absent without leave May 1, 1864.
Allen, W H.	Nov. 20, 1861	Belongs to Fifth Tennessee Infantry. Reported to this company for duty while in West Tennessee.
Archer, William		
Alexander, Van.		
Adams, William.		
Blythe, J. W.		Killed at Tishomingo Creek, July 14, 1864.
Brogden, F. M.	Nov. 22, 1861	Absent, sick, August 20, 1862.
Blake, Leonidas		
Blake, W P		
Blake, James		
Bowden, John		
Blanchett, J. H.		
Biles, G. W.		
Blythe, C T.		
Bell, T. N		
Ballard, B. F	Nov. 22, 1861	Dismounted by enemy at Union City March 31, 1862. Transferred to sharp-shooters September 1, 1862.
Bishop, ——		Wounded at Fort Heiman, Tenn, 1862.
Boyd, Joseph		
Beard, Joseph		
Bizentine, Monroe		
Burton, Jefferson L.	Oct. 15, 1861	Left at home, sick, February 15, 1862.
Bridges, Porter		
Beard, Samuel		

Name.	Date of Enlistment.	Remarks.
Bizentine, William..		
Burton, C. W.	Nov. 1, 1861	Detailed as teamster October 15, 1862.
Burton, Charles..		
Bridges, Pearl.		
Blythe, Calvin T.		
Biggs, B. M.		Mortally wounded at Davis's Bridge, 1862.
Coffman, W. M.	Nov. 15, 1861	Absent, sick, in Henry County, Tenn, March 20, 1864.
Cox, M. M	Mar. 26, 1863	Rejoined February 25, 1864.
Cook, Z. T..	Sept. 21, 1863	Absent without leave March 25, 1864.
Cook, J. D..		
Collins, J. E...		
Chiles, James H.		
Caton, George T.		
Callaway, J. E.		
Carter, Archie...		
Conssy, J. M..		
Calhoun, Charles		
Cox, Asa...w.		
Carter, A. W.;	Oct. 14, 1861	On detached service (Gen. Villipigue), October 20, 1863.
Coffman, William..		
Collins, Richard...		
Cayton, Dick		
Coleman, T. T		Mortally wounded at Okolona Feb. 22, 1864. Died March 7, 1864.
Clark, T. H.	Nov. 28, 1861	Left sick near Brownsville April 15, 1862.
Dalton, C F....	Mar. 10, 1862	Absent without leave in Calloway County, Ky., May 1, 1864.
Dalton, John W	Sept. 25, 1863	Absent, sick, in Calloway County, Ky., March 5, 1864.
Douglass, J. M.	Dec 31, 1861	Detailed as regimental blacksmith February 22, 1864.
Dunlap, R. A.....		

Duncan, James
Darby, Rich.
Dent, Samuel
Daniel, William................ Killed at Britton's Lane September 1, 1862.
Eseridge, J. R. .... Died at Irby Mills January 27, 1864.
Erwin, T. A. .... Killed at Harrisburg July 14, 1864.
Elderidge, W. F.
Field, H. H .... May 20, 1861 Absent, wounded, from March 21 to May 12, 1864.
Field, ——...................... Nov. 28, 1861 Detailed as teamster January 1, 1862.
Griffin, T. J.
Granger, J. F .... Nov. 20, 1861 Absent, sick, March 25, 1864.
Grubbs, Thomas
Grogan, T. R.
Grogan, J. P.
Guthrie, William F.
Grogan, T. K.
Gwynn, James
Gilbert, R. M. .... Nov. 26, 1861 Transferred to Company H February 29, 1864.
Higgs, James .... " " Died in the service.
Holt, W. B.
Howard, F. L.
Humphrey, Wm. M........ May 20, 1861 Absent, wounded, March 21, 1864.
Haynes, S. P. .... May 20, 1861 Rejoined February 25, 1864.
Hicks, A. J. .... Sept. 25, 1863 Absent without leave March 25, 1864.
Harmon, J. K. P.
Hudspeth, George
Hicks, Nathan.
Hicks, James
Harris, Charles
Harris, G.

Name.	Date of Enlistment.	Remarks.
Hutchins, Major		
Holt, W B		
Jones, J J	Nov. 1, 1861	Captured February 20, 1864.
Johnston, J J		
Johnston, F F		
Jones, J W		
Jenkins, Joseph		
Jenkins, William		
Jenkins, Monroe		
Julien, J N	Dec. 10, 1861	Transferred to Company H February 29, 1864.
Korn, C H		
Kelso, L C	Sept. 21, 1863	Absent without leave March 25, 1864.
Lassiter, R C	Nov. 20, 1861	Left sick near Grenada February 12, 1864.
Lemonds, D W	Nov. 28, 1861	{ Detailed as stoker for regiment blacksmith. Absent with leave May 4, 1864.
Littleton, J F		
Lambrick, Richard		
Looney, Jesse C	Nov. 14, 1861	Left sick in West Tennessee September 20, 1863.
Lowden, James		
Looney, Thomas		
Manley, N E		
Mctehee, J W		
Martin, John W		
McConnell, W C		
McConnell, J W		
McConnell, W W		
Morris, W D		
McClure,		

Name	Date	Remarks
Miller, William		
McFarland, William		
Miller, Pleas		
Morris, H. T.		
Moore, Joseph T.	Nov. 28, 1861	Left sick near Humboldt June 1, 1862.
McFarland, R. J.		
Milton, William		
Meek, William		
Mitchell, P.		Killed near Oxford, Miss., 1861.
Mayo, W. G.	Mar. 17, 1862	Transferred to Alabama Regiment October 25, 1862.
Neal, James	Dec. 10, 1861	Transferred to Company H February 29, 1864.
Nunn, James	Nov. 9, 1861	Detailed as teamster December, 1863.
Nelson, William	Apr. 22, 1863	Transferred to Company H February 29, 1864.
Nelson, H.	Mar. 23, 1863	Transferred to Company H February 29, 1864.
Olive, James	Nov. 22, 1861	Wounded and left near Panola May 22, 1863.
Palmer, John		Killed near Oxford, Miss., 1864.
Poore, M. F.		
Paschal, T. L.	May 20, 1861	Absent without leave May 1, 1864.
Page, James		
Payner, H.	Nov. 22, 1861	Left sick near Jackson May, 1862, and reported dead.
Paschal, J. F.		
Renfroe, George W.	Oct. 18, 1862	Left sick near Trenton, Tenn., May 28, 1862.
Renfroe, Jack	Nov. 9, 1861	Detailed as teamster October, 1862.
Rigsby, J. M.		
Rainey, J. B.		
Rushing, ——		
Rigsby, Sam		
Reynolds, ——		

Name.	Date of Enlistment.	Remarks.
Ross, Alex		Died in hospital at Grenada.
Rigsby, L. J.	Nov. 2, 1861	Left sick near Brownsville May, 1862.
Simmons, T. C.	Feb. 23, 1861	Left with wounded at Corinth, as surgeon, October 4, 1862.
Simmons, W. H.		

Privates.

Name.	Date of Enlistment.	Remarks.
Shipley, J. H.	May 22, 1862	Absent sick since September 22, 1862.
Stubblefield, W. B.	June 1, 1862	Left sick near Panola February 6, 1864.
Stubblefield, W. L.	Jan. 1, 1862	Absent with leave since April 25, 1864.
Stubblefield, R.W., Sr.	Jan. 1, 1861	Absent wounded, March 21, 1864, to May 12, 1864.
Stubblefield, R.W., Jr.	Sept. 25, 1862	Absent sick from March 25, 1864, to May 12, 1864.
Scarborough, G. T.	Sept. 1, 1863	Absent without leave April 15, 1864.
Steele, J. W.	Sept. 17, 1861	Absent without leave May 1, 1864.
Seawright, John L.		
Stone, James W.	Jan. 1, 1862	Detailed at Gen. Villipigue's head-quarters.
Sproul, S. B.		
Short, ...		
Stites, John		
Stewart, J. H.		Mortally wounded at Tishomingo Creek June 10, 1864.
Seawright, J. L.	Nov. 28, 1861	Rejoined April 1, 1864.
Tandy, C. W.		
Thurston, W. H.	Nov. 8, 1861	Rejoined February 18, 1864.
Taylor, T. H.		
Todd, Rufus		
Taylor, J. C.		Died in prison.

Name.		Remarks.
Vandyck, W. O.		Sept. 20, 1863 Left sick near Sardis January 1864.
Vandyck, John		
Wakeland, H. F.		
Wright, J. H.		
Walker, J. H.		May 20, 1864 Wounded and left in hospital at Okolona February 22, 1864.
Wilkins, John		
Warnick,		
Wright, Leon		
Wright, S. C.		
Wheeler,		
Wesson, Alex.		
Wilson, W. S.		Nov. 28, 1864 Absent sick July 1864.

COMPANY H.

Name.	Rank.	Date of Enlistment.	Remarks.
H. C. McCutchen	Captain.		Wounded and captured at Lamar, Miss., Nov. 8, 1862.
J. A. Jenkins	Lieutenant.		Wounded at Britton's Lane September 1, 1862. Captured November 10, 1862, and died in prison.
James Williams	Lieutenant.		Afterward Captain in another regiment.
E. T. Hollis	Lieutenant.		Wounded and captured at Lamar, Miss, November 8, 1862.
W. R. Jones	Lieutenant.		
W. E. Martin	Sergeant.	Dec. 10, 1861	Absent without leave from December 25, 1862, to April 1, 1864.
J. A. Nowlin	Sergeant.		
T. J. Franklin	Sergeant.		
A. H. Johnson	Sergeant.		
J. W. Mock	Corporal.		

Name.	Rank.	Date of Enlistment.	Remarks.
J. M. Goolsby	Corporal.	Dec. 10, 1861	Absent without leave from December 25, 1862, to April 1, 1864.
W G. Barber	Corporal.	Dec. 10, 1861	Absent without leave from December 8, 1862, to April 1, 1864.
R. A. Rosa	Corporal.	Dec. 10, 1861	Left at Corinth October 4, 1862.
George Muse	Corporal.	Dec. 10, 1861	
Samuel Anderson	Corporal.	Dec. 10, 1861	Detailed as courier for Gen. Rust, 1862.

Privates.

Name.	Date of Enlistment.	Remarks.
Adams W C	Dec 10, 1861	Absent without leave from December 7, 1862, to April 1, 1864.
Adams, J. B.	Dec. 10, 1861	Left sick at Jackson, Miss., May 29, 1862. Absent without leave from December 7, 1862, to April 1, 1864.
Adams, William A.	Dec. 10, 1861	Absent without leave from December 10, 1862, to April 1, 1864. Killed at Brice's Cross Roads June 10, 1864.
Adkins, J. C.		
Blackburn, J. M.	Dec. 10, 1861	Absent without leave from December 8, 1862, to April 1, 1864.
Barger, J. N.		
Butts, W C	Dec. 10, 1861	Absent without leave from March 12, 1862, to April 1, 1864.
Baldridge, J. L.	Dec. 10, 1861	Left sick at Trenton May 27, 1862.
Bondurant, J. J. C.		Wounded at Harrisburg July 14, 1864.
Barrett, J. W.		
Boyd, Spencer		
Blankenship, J. W.		
Boon, J. E.		
Baker, R. A. E	Dec. 10, 1862	Detailed as courier for Gen. Villipigue October, 1864.
Carroll, W L	Dec. 10, 1861	Discharged for disability August 2, 1862.

Name	Date	Remarks
Cravens, J		Absent without leave from September 1, 1863, to April 1, 1864.
Cravens, John J		Wounded at Brice's Cross Roads June 10, 1864.
Cantrell, J. J	Dec. 10, 1861	Wounded at Harrisburg July 14, 1864.
Curry, S. H	Dec. 10, 1861	Detailed as blacksmith, 1862. Absent without leave from November 28, 1862, to April 1, 1864.
Chambers, H. D		
Cavitt, Bennett		
Carroll, John		Wounded at Medon or Britton's Lane, 1862.
Davis, F. M	Dec. 10, 1861	Left sick at Ripley, June 4, 1862. Went home and was forced to take Federal oath of allegiance.
Drake, J. W		
Dent, Samuel		Killed at Britton's Lane September 1, 1862.
Eskridge, J. R	Dec. 10, 1861	Absent without leave from December 13, 1862, to April, 1864. Killed at Harrisburg July 14, 1864.
Eskridge, J. W		
Freeman, W. A	Dec. 10, 1861	Died at home April 1, 1862.
Farmer, J. B		Absent without leave from September 1, 1863, to April 1, 1864. Wounded at Britton's Lane September 1, 1862.
Franklin, T. A		
Farmer, W. H. H	Dec. 10, 1861	Left sick at Canton Station, Tenn., May 25, 1862.
Gilbert, R. M		
Gatus, W. M		
Griggs, Barney		
Glenn, J. A		
Glimp, J. A		
Glass, J. C		
Goodsby, J. M		
Gates, N. J		
Govan, F. M	Dec. 10, 1861	Left sick at Spring Creek May 4, 1862.

Name.	Date of Enlistment.	Remarks.
Harris, J. M.	Dec. 10, 1861	Detailed as courier for Gen. Rust, 1862.
Haralson, J. H.	Apr. 10, 1861	Went home sick from Paris December 20, 1861.
Howard, James	Apr. 10, 1861	{ Left sick February, 1862, white-swelling in thigh. Absent without leave from May 29, 1862, to April 1, 1864.
Hazlewood, John	Dec. 10, 1861	{ Absent without leave from December 7, 1862, to April 1, 1864. Wounded at Harrisburg July 14, 1864.
Hutchins, F. M.	Dec. 10, 1861	Absent without leave from December 12, 1862, to April 1, 1864.
Hamilton, J.	Apr. 10, 1861	{ Discharged May 22, 1862, over thirty-five (?) years of age. Reported again for duty April 1, 1864.
Hilliard, Daniel	Dec. 10, 1861	Absent without leave from December 7, 1862, to April 1, 1864.
Higgs, James N. B.		Died in the service at Henry Station, March 26, 1862.
Huskeith, J. L.	Apr. 10, 1861	Discharged for sickness May 22, 1862.
Hollis, J. M.	Jan. 13, 1862	Left near Holly Springs September 28, 1862, wounded in the foot.
Julian, J. N		Wounded at Harrisburg July 14, 1864.
Julian, J. J.		
Jones, James		Wounded at Brice's Cross Roads June 10, 1864.
Johnson, M. H	Dec. 10, 1861	Left at Trenton June 4, 1862.
Johnson, A.	Dec. 10, 1861	Detailed as courier for Gen. Villipique, 1862.
Johnson, W. M		{ Detailed as wagoner, Col. Jackson's head-quarters, 1862. Died December 28, 1864.
Kingston, E. W		
Landrum, James	Dec. 10, 1861	Left at Cassville May 16, 1862.
Lynn, W. H	Dec. 10, 1861	Absent without leave from June 4, 1862, to April 1, 1864.
Lynn, Henry		Wounded and captured at Lamar, Miss. November 8, 1862.
Meek, J. W.		Killed near Oxford, 1864.
Meek, William		Absent without leave from November 12, 1862, to April 1, 1864.
McBride, D. J		

Name	Date	Remarks
Mitchell, R. H.		Detailed as courier for Gen. Rust, 1862. Wounded at Sulphur Trestle, Ala., 1864.
McNamee, Samuel	Apr. 18, 1862	Absent without leave December 25, 1862, to April 1, 1864.
Mosely, W. T.	Apr. 25, 1861	Absent by permission May 11, 1864, to hunt his stolen horse.
Mayo, W. G.	Dec. 10, 1861	Absent since April 15, 1864.
Morton, W. E.		
Melton, W. L.	Dec. 10, 1861	Left at Cassville May 16, 1862.
Montgomery, W. B.	Dec. 10, 1861	Discharged at Trenton May 22, 1862.
Nelson, Hugh	Mar. 1, 1863	Detailed to drive wagon May 11, 1864.
Nelson, William	Apr. 26, 1862	Detailed to drive wagon May 11, 1864.
Nowlin, J. A. P.		Wounded at Brice's Cross Roads.
Proctor, R.		
Parks, W. G.		
Palmer, J. K.		
Palmer, D. E.		Killed near Oxford, Miss., 1862.
Riley, James		
Rose, R. A.		
Roberts, R. E.		
Roberts, J. H. N.		
Ross, J. Alexander		Wounded and captured at Lamar, Miss. November 8, 1862. Died in hospital at Grenada, Miss.
Sims, R. H.	Dec. 10, 1861	Captured by enemy at Union City March 1, 1862.
Stewart, J. H.	Dec. 10, 1861	Wounded severely at Britton's Lane September 1, 1862, and left on the field. Wounded at Brice's Cross Roads and died December, 1864.
Speed, H. M.	Dec. 10, 1861	Detailed as courier for Gen. Rust, 1862.
Stull, Mark	Dec. 10, 1861	Went home sick from Como May 4, 1862.
Smith, J. A.		Wounded at Harrisburg July 14, 1864.
Thompson, J. T.		
Talley, J. E.		

Name.	Date of Enlistment.	Remarks.
Taylor, Joseph C	Dec. 10, 1861	Captured August 9, 1863, and died in prison.
Thomas, J. E.		
Travis, T. W		Wounded at Brice's Cross Roads June 10, 1864.
Travis, James		
Ward, J. J	Dec. 10, 1862	Discharged at Trenton May 22, 1862—over thirty-five years of age
Willson, John	Dec. 10, 1862	Died at Paris, Tenn, February 28, 1862.
Weatherly, J. W.		
Ward, Sim		
Ward, C. J		
Ward, W H		
Watts, Bowling		
Williams, Daniel	Dec. 10, 1861	Absent without leave from December 13, 1862, to April 1, 1864.
Williams, J. T		
Winston, S. A	Dec. 10, 1861	Absent without leave from December 13, 1862, to April 1, 1864. Wounded at Brice's Cross Roads June 10, 1864.

COMPANY I.

Name.	Rank.	Date of Enlistment.	Remarks.
Lafayette Hill.	Captain.		Captured and shot while a prisoner near Covington, Tenn., September 30, 1862, but recovered.
J. R. Alexander	Captain.		Wounded and captured at Lamar, Miss., Nov. 8, 1862.
W P. Malone.	Lieutenant.		Wounded at Hermando, Miss., June 19, 1863. Absent on sick leave May 11, 1864, since July 19, 1863.
John T. Douglass.	Lieutenant.		
Philip A. Fisher	Lieutenant.		
Henry D. Smith	Lieutenant.		

Name		Date of Enlistment	Remarks
E. M. Downing	Lieutenant.		
C. C. Dodson	Sergeant.	Mar. 7, 1861	Transferred from Second Alabama Regiment May 11, 1862. Wounded at Britton's Lane September 1, 1862.
John W. Shelton	Sergeant.	Mar. 15, 1862	Wounded at Harrisburg July 14, 1864.
H. P. Colton	Sergeant.	Mar. 15, 1862	Absent without leave May 2, 1864.
John C. Pace	Sergeant.	Mar. 16, 1862	Absent without leave May 2, 1864.
John D. Smith	Sergeant.	Mar. 15, 1862	Absent without leave October 17, 1862.
W. H. Frazer	Sergeant.	Mar. 15, 1862	Absent, wounded, May 5, 1864.
Joseph Alston	Sergeant.		
Samuel Long	Sergeant.		Transferred to Company K October 6, 1862. Rejoined April 15, 1864.
G. W. Overall	Corporal.		
A. W. Walk	Corporal.		
J. M. Barrett	Corporal.		
R. C. Smith	Corporal.		
William Sanford	Corporal.		

Privates.

Name	Date of Enlistment	Remarks
Adkins, Dick		Died in prison at Alton, Ill.
Alston, Philip H.		
Armour, Capt.		Killed at Collierville October 11, 1863.
Brown, Joseph	May 15, 1861	Left dismounted near Ripley May 6, 1864. Killed at Harrisburg July 14, 1864.
Bringle, Thomas		
Bringle, J. H		
Bringle, T. H.		Captured at Britton's Lane September 1, 1862.
Bledsoe, Cyrus		

Name.	Date of Enlistment.	Remarks.
Burleson, W. L.	Mar. 15, 1862	Absent, sick, with leave October 30, 1862.
Barrett, J. M.	Mar. 15, 1862	Absent without leave May 2, 1864.
Caples, William		
Cannon, Henry		
Cage, W. H.		Killed at Tishomingo Creek June 10 1864.
Caraway, W. T.		
Caples, Van	Mar. 18, 1862	Teamster in Assistant Quartermaster's Department May 11, 1864.
Clark, J. D.	June 16, 1863	Transferred from Fourth Tennessee Volunteers June 16, 1862. Killed at Harrisburg June 14, 1864.
Clark, J. S.	July 16, 1864	Transferred from Fourth Tennessee Volunteers June 16, 1862.
Colton, R. J.	May 25, 1862	Absent without leave May 9, 1864.
Coats, Newton	Apr. 15, 1864	Absent without leave May 2, 1864.
Coats, Thomas		
Coats, Solomon		
Coats, Wilson	July 17, 1862	Rejoined April 17, 1864.
Coats, James		
I. Clement		
Collier, Joseph T.		Rejoined April 15, 1864.
Coward, William S.		
Cockrill, William		
Crawfield, Isaac		
Collier, Pate		
Davis, J. F.		
Ducus, W. C.		
Dobson, J. E.	May 11, 1862	Absent without leave May 2, 1864. Transferred from Fourth Tennessee Volunteers May 23, 1862. Wounded and captured at Lamar November 8, 1862. On special service May 11, 1864. Killed at Harrisburg July 14, 1864.
Douglass, J. A.		

Dunn, James	Killed at Britton's Lane September 1, 1862.
Dillahunty, James	Wounded at Britton's Lane September 1, 1862.
Dodson, Thomas	
Ervin, R. P.	
Evans, E. J.	
Edwards, William	
Fisher, C. J	On special service May 2, 1864. Wounded and captured at Lamar, Miss., November 8, 1862.
Ferrell, B. H.	Sept. 24, 1863 Absent, sick, May 2, 1864.
Ferrell, W. S.	
French, John	
Flanigan, Isaac W.	Wounded and captured at Lamar, Miss., November 8, 1862.
Foster, W H	
Fridle, A. W.	
Garthy, William	
Goforth, R.	
Glendale, O. O.	Apr. 15, 1864 Absent, wounded, May 2, 1864.
Green, D.	
Grant, James T	Mar. 15, 1862 In commissary department with regiment May 11, 1864.
Guthrie, William	Wounded in service.
Grimes, Nathan	
Grant, G. W.	Died in service.
Goss, J. A.	Aug. 17, 1862 Absent, sick, with leave, October 30, 1862.
Haynie, A. P.	
Hartsfield, R. F.	Apr. 15, 1864 Absent without leave May 2, 1862.
Holtshouser, H.	
Hutton, T. H.	Mar. 18, 1862 Rejoined April 2, 1864.
Haynie, William T.	Mar. 15, 1862 **Absent** on special service October 30, 1862.
Harris, William	
Hughlett, J. A.	

Name.	Date of Enlistment.	Remarks.
Hall, William		
Hyndman, Alex.		
Jourdan, S. B.		
Jones, H. W. B.	May 15, 1862	Died in service September 1, 1862, near Senatobia, Miss
Jones, R.	May 10, 1863	Absent without leave May 2, 1864.
Krobbs, Henry	July 22, 1862	Nurse for wounded at Tupelo May 11, 1864.
Kurtz, John		
Kinny, Isaac C.		
Lauderdale, J. D. H.	Mar. 15, 1862	Absent without leave October 10, 1862.
Lamphier, W. Mc		
Lippman, Alexander		Special service May 2, 1864. Wounded at Harrisburg July 14, 1864.
Long, Samuel	Mar. 15, 1862	Transferred to Company K October 11, 1862. Rejoined April 15, 1864.
Lock, J. M.	Mar. 15, 1862	Absent without leave October 30, 1862. Rejoined April 15, 1864.
Lauderdale, Josiah		
Littleton, William	Mar. 15, 1862	Absent without leave. Captured near Memphis October, 1862.
Marsh, Samuel		
Max, F. M.	Mar. 18, 1862	Absent, sick, May 2, 1864.
McDaniel, E.	Mar. 15, 1862	Rejoined April 15, 1862.
McFadden, R.		
McGregor, R. R.	Mar. 15, 1862	Courier to Gen. Villipigue October 30, 1862. Absent without leave May 11, 1864.
Montgomery, Alex.		
Montgomery, Robert		
Montgomery, S W.	Apr. 15, 1862	Absent with leave May 11, 1864.
Morgan, F. A.	May 23, 1861	Transferred from Company C, Ninth Tennessee, May 22, 1862.
Musey, F M.	May 15, 1862	Absent without leave since May 2, 1864.
Myers, A. A.		

Name	Date	Remarks
Miller, G.,......		
Mehagan, Robert		
May, Daniel A.	Jan. 23, 1863	Killed near Pontotoc February 23, 1864.
Munford, E. H..		Died at Charleston, Miss., January 24, 1863.
Morgan, E. J...	Mar. 15, 1862	Discharged from disability October 17, 1862.
Normend, Ellis		Died in service.
Overall, J. P.	May 15, 1862	{ Wounded and captured at Lamar November 8, 1862. Rejoined April 15, 1864.
Overall, T. C......		
Owen, J. H..		Died in prison.
Owen, Newton....		Killed at Harrisburg July 14, 1864.
Petty, Nathan...		Wounded at Shiloh April 6, 1862.
Peeler, William S.		
Plueson, William..		
Richardson, M. T.		
Rose, R. A.	Mar. 15, 1862	{ Absent without leave August 10, 1862. Captured at Covington, Tenn., September 30, 1862.
Roberts, B. F.....	May 18, 1862	In Quartermaster's Department with the regiment May 11, 1864.
Ross, F. M.		In Quarantine Department with Jackson's Brigade May 11, 1864.
Rutherford, F. H.		
Rutherford, R....		
Rose, Lee W		
Rose, Samuel		
Riley, James G...		Wounded at Sulphur Trestle, Ala., 1864.
Roe, John...		
Ridgeway, D. A. .		
Sanford, Bailey..		
Sanford, William.		
Sanford, J. R.		
Smith, H. Y....		

Name.	Date of Enlistment.	Remarks.
Smith, W D, Sr.		
Smith, W. D, Jr.	May 15, 1861	Wounded at Prairie Mound February 1, 1864; and May 11, 1864, at Starkville hospital.
Smith, A. W	May 15, 1861	Absent with leave May 11, 1864.
Smith, J. D		At Alton, Ill., United States Military Prison May 11, 1864.
Smith, J. M.	May 15, 1862	Wounded and captured at Lamar, Miss, November 8, 1862. Rejoined May 11, 1864.
Smith, R. L		Wounded and captured at Lamar, Miss, November 8, 1862.
Smith, R. C		
Smith, W. A		Wounded at Tishomingo Creek June 10, 1864.
Smith, J. H		
Spencer, John		Killed at Tishomingo Creek.
Spencer, S		
Stone, J. J	Sept. 1, 1862	Absent without leave May 11, 1864. Wounded at Harrisburg July 14, 1864.
Somerville, John		
Steel, Thomas		Killed at La Fayette Station, Tenn., 1862.
Shankle, Jasper		
Smith, Peyton J	May 15, 1862	Absent with leave and captured at Covington, Tenn., October, 1862. Wounded at Hernando June 19, 1863.
Smith, R. W		
Smith, Albert C		
St. Secre, Frank		
Shankle, Ro.		
Taylor, J. H		Discharged from disability September, 1862.
Taylor, Samuel L		
Taylor, W M		
Turner, R.		
Turner, B. S.		

Turner, Robert		
Turner, J. B.	June 17, 1862	Absent, sick, October 30, 1862.
Trantham, Newton J.		Wounded and captured at Lamar, Miss., November 8, 1862.
Tims, Frank		
Towell, Isaac		
Tarbro, L. B.		
Tarbro, J. H.		Died at Fort Pillow, 1862.
Upchurch, James		
Upchurch, William G.		
Walton, W. H.		
White, R. W.		
Warmouth, R. H.	Apr. 15, 1864	Absent, sick, May 5, 1864.
Wormouth, T. P.		
Wortham, Nathan	Mar. 15, 1862	Absent without leave October 30, 1862.
Walk, A. W.		Wounded at Collierville, October 11, 1863.
Wood, John W.		
Wilson, J. D.		Wounded at Oxford, Miss., 1863.
Wray, Joseph		Wounded at Britton's Lane. Died in prison.
Winbourne, J. T.		
Walton, George W.		Wounded and captured at Lamar November 8, 1862.
Williams, Nathan		Wounded and captured at Lamar November 8, 1862.
Yarbrough, John A.		Wounded and captured at Lamar November 8, 1862.
Yarbrough, S. B.		Absent without leave May 2, 1864.

Note by Orderly Sergeant.—The above-named I. Hugelett and I. Clement left the command in Tipton County, Tenn, on the 6th of June last, on the march, by permission of Capt. L. Hill, neither of them being able for duty; and, as I am advised, are not able for duty at this time, both having chronic diseases.

Company K.

Name.	Rank.	Date of Enlistment.	Remarks.
Samuel T. Taylor	Captain.	Mar. 18, 1862	Resigned Oct. 17, 1862. Absent with leave Oct. 30, 1862.
William F. Broadnax	Lieutenant.		
J. J. Mullins	Lieutenant.	Mar. 18, 1862	Resigned October 27, 1862.
W. L. Barleson.	Lieutenant.		
H. H. Elean.	Sergeant.	Mar. 18, 1862	Transferred to Company B. August 21, 1862.
J. R. Cofield.	Sergeant.		
William Delaschmit.	Sergeant.	Mar. 18, 1862	Absent without leave October 30, 1862.
S. L. Taylor.	Sergeant.	Mar. 18, 1862	Absent, sick, October 30, 1862.
W. J. Westmoreland.	Corporal.	Mar. 18, 1862	Transferred to Company B August 18, 1862.
R. Stephens.	Corporal.		
J. L. Atkins.	Corporal.		
T. H. Hutton.	Corporal.	Mar. 18, 1862	Absent, sick, October 30, 1862.

Privates.

Name.	Date of Enlistment.	Remarks.
Bass, J. C.	Mar. 18, 1862	Transferred to Company B. August 21, 1862.
Bradsher, L. D.		
Bradsher, W.	Mar. 18, 1862	Absent, sick, October 30, 1862.
Claiborne, J. M.	Mar. 18, 1862	Transferred to Company B. August 21, 1862.
Claiborne, J. A.	Mar. 18, 1862	Transferred to Company L. August 21, 1862.
Coats, G. G.	Mar. 18, 1862	Discharged July 18, 1862.
Cofield, J. A.	Mar. 18, 1862	Absent without leave October 30, 1862.
Chambers, S. C.	Mar. 18, 1862	Transferred to Company B. August 21, 1862.
Capels, W.		
Capels, W. G.	Mar. 18, 1862	Absent, sick, October 30, 1862.

Name		
Bodson, T. C.		Captured at Old Lamar, Miss, November 8, 1862.
Bunn, James		
Belaschnit, G. B.	Mar. 18, 1862	Died August 4, 1862.
Edmonds, J. W.		
Ekran, A. L.	Mar. 18, 1862	Transferred to Company B August 21, 1862.
Ekran, W. H.	Mar. 18, 1862	Discharged June 8, 1862.
French, H. J.		
French, J. A.		
Field, J. B.		
Griffin, W. L.		
Grimes, N. W.		
George, William		
J. C. Goodbread		Died in hospital about December 1, 1863.
Hunt, J. H.	Mar. 18, 1862	Transferred to Company B August 21, 1862.
Hardin, W. P.	Mar. 18, 1862	Discharged July 18, 1862.
Hilliard, W. C.	Mar. 18, 1862	Transferred to Company B August 21, 1862.
Harris, W. R.		
Hamilton, O. E.		
Jordan, T. A.	Mar. 18, 1862	Transferred to Company B August 21, 1862.
Jones, W. L. T.		
Lloyd, J. L.	Mar. 18, 1862	Died April 25, 1862.
Loving, H. W.		
Long, Samuel	Mar. 15, 1862	Transferred from Company I October 11, 1862.
Maclin, J. T.	Mar. 18, 1862	Captured at Ripley and paroled, 1862.
Maclin, J. C.		
Max, F. M.		
McAlilly, F. M.		
McAlilly, J. M.		
Montgomery, S. W.		
Musey, Francis		

Name.	Date of Enlistment.	Remarks.
Morton, F. G	Mar. 18, 1862	Absent, detailed to wait on sick October 30, 1862.
Mason, F. Y	Mar. 18, 1862	Transferred to Company B August 18, 1862.
McKinney, J. C.	Mar. 18, 1862	Died April 30, 1862.
Malone, J. W		
Newton, F. G. W		
Overall, G. W		
Overall, T. C.		
Poindexter, C. C.	Mar. 18, 1862	Transferred to Company B August 21, 1862.
Poston, T. H		Captured at Old Lamar November 8, 1862.
Petty, N	Mar. 18, 1862	Absent, sick, October 30, 1862.
Rose, R. H.		
Roberts, J. B.		
Ross, F M		
Stewart, H	Mar. 18, 1862	Absent without leave October 30, 1862.
Shepperd, H		
Smith, S. M.		
Tims, B. T		
Tims, J		
Taylor, J. M.		
Whitley, Joseph	May 13, 1862	Discharged October 25, 1862.
Wallace, William	Mar. 18, 1862	Transferred to Company B August 21, 1862.
Wharton, Joseph		Killed at Salem October 8, 1863.
Young, W L		
Young, L. F		
Younghlool, H. A.		
Yandall, W. M	Mar. 18, 1862	Discharged September 24, 1862.

COMPANY L.

Name.	Rank.	Date of Enlistment.	Remarks.
James A. Taylor	Captain.	Apr. 30, 1864	{ Absent on surgeon's certificate October 30, 1862. Re- signed in 1862, about November.
Alex. Duckworth	Captain.	" "	Wounded at Collierville October 11, 1863.
Charles S. Taliaferro	Lieutenant.	" "	
A. Austin	Lieutenant.	" "	
Frank Pugh	Lieutenant.	April 4, 1862	Promoted January 12, 1864.
Wm. Witherspoon	Lieutenant.	" "	Discharged in fall of 1862.
E. R. Crandel	Sergeant.	" "	Wounded at Harrisburg July 14, 1864.
R. D. Grove	Sergeant.	" "	
Thomas E. Rooks	Sergeant.	Apr. 30, 1862	Absent with leave May 11, 1864.
J. C. W. Cobb	Sergeant.	" "	
Samuel A. Taylor	Sergeant.	" "	
J. M. Currie	Sergeant.	Apr. 4, 1862	Transferred from Company F August 27, 1862.
Ed Freeman	Sergeant.	" "	
M. H. Dupree	Corporal.	" "	Killed July 13, 1864, near Harrisburg, Miss.
W. L. Barnes	Corporal.	" "	Killed July 13, 1864, near Harrisburg, Miss.
Thomas E. Nelson	Corporal.	" "	Detailed as bugler August 1, 1863.
W. P. Steel	Corporal.	" "	
W. H. Dupree	Corporal.	Apr. 30, 1862	Detailed as wheelwright February 5, 1864.

Privates.

Name.	Date of Enlistment.	Remarks.
Allison, B. W.	Apr. 30, 1862	Absent, sick, May 11, 1864.
Anthony, William T.		

Name.	Date of Enlistment.	Remarks.
Anthony, William I.	Apr. 30, 1862	Absent on sick leave October 30, 1862.
Bancom, J. T.	Apr. 30, 1862	Absent on surgeon's certificate October 30, 1862.
Branch, Hugh		
Brantley, S. N.		
Bauch, J. V.	Feb. 6, 1863	Rejoined February 10, 1864.
Currie, J. M.		
Currie, W. Thomas	Feb. 1, 1864	Sent to Brownsville May, 1864, to guard ambulance.
Claiborne, John A	Mar. 18, 1862	Transferred from Company K August 27, 1862.
Clay, Joseph W	Oct. 1, 1862	Detailed as courier May 11, 1864.
Coleman, L. R.	Nov. 1, 1862	Detailed teamster December 20, 1863. Absent without leave February 29, 1864.
Coleman, R. M.		
Castillon, James	Apr. 30, 1862	Rejoined April 1, 1864.
Castillon, John		
Cobb, W. T.	Apr. 30, 1862	Absent without leave October 30, 1862. Rejoined April 1, 1864.
Cobb, S. A.	Apr. 30, 1862	Rejoined April 1, 1864.
Cole, P. H.	Apr. 1, 1864	Absent with leave May 11, 1864.
Coltart, R. M.		
Connor, C. C.		
Chrisman, W. J		
DeLeach, Arthur	Apr. 30, 1862	Absent with leave October 30, 1862.
Duckworth, John C.		
Davis, Thomas		
Drake, W. Baxter		Captured at Britton's Lane September 1, 1862.
Davis, Henry		
Brennan, J. C.	Oct. 28, 1862	
Drake, R. B.	Apr. 30, 1862	Absent without leave October 30, 1862.

Name	Date	Remarks
Fox, C. H.	Apr. 4, 1864	Transferred from Company F August 27, 1862. Absent without leave October 30, 1862.
Fortune, B. W.	Apr. 30, 1862	Rejoined February 10, 1864. Wounded at Harrisburg July 14, 1864.
Freeman, W. G.	Apr. 30, 1862	Detailed as courier for Gen Villipigue October 30, 1862. Wounded and left near Prairie Mound February 21, 1864.
George, William		Died about November 16, 1863, at Irby's Mills
Green, John A. V.	Apr. 30, 1862	On provost duty in regiment since November 20, 1863.
Green, Carlos E.		
Grove, R. R.		
Garrett, W. R.	Apr. 30, 1862	Transferred from Company D, 1862.
Groves, Reuben		Absent without leave October 30, 1862.
Graves, A. J.	Apr. 30, 1862	Absent without leave April 30, 1864.
Grant, B. F.	Apr. 30, 1862	Relieved by substitute, 1862.
Harris, H. H.		
Holland, J. L.		Absent without leave October 30, 1862. Rejoined April 1, 1864. Discharged because of ill health.
Hopkins, Joseph L.		
Herron, J. W.		
Hawkins, L. B.		
Hodgkins, R. D.	Apr. 30, 1862	Absent without leave October 30, 1862. Rejoined April 1, 1864.
Hughes, B. F.		
Hughes, William	Apr. 30, 1862	Rejoined February 1, 1864.
Hopkins, Samuel F.	Apr. 30, 1862	Wounded at Medon August 31, 1862.
Hooper, James		While lieutenant was wounded April 6, 1862, at Shiloh. Joined as private after recovery.
Hotchkiss, S. B.		
Hotchkiss, R. L.		
Hughes, John		
Jacocks, Joseph		

Name.	Date of Enlistment.	Remarks.
Jeffries, G. W.	Apr. 30, 1862	Absent, sick, with leave, October 30, 1862.
Jones, William	Apr. 30, 1862	Absent on surgeon's certificate October 30, 1862.
Klyce, William		
King, D. N.		
Lynn, William E.	Apr. 20, 1862	Transferred from Company I August 27, 1862.
Loving, A. B.		
Lea, J. M.	Apr. 30, 1862	Rejoined January 15, 1864.
Lea, H. M.		
Lea, J. G.		
Lea, Jere		
McLeod, John P.		
Marbry, P. H.	Apr. 1, 1864	Absent, sick, May 11, 1864.
Mann, J. A.		
Moore, J. L.	Apr. 30, 1862	Absent without leave October 30, 1862. Rejoined April 1, 1864.
Moore, C. H.	Apr. 30, 1862	Absent on surgeon's certificate October 30, 1862.
Mebane, Robert		Wounded at Collierville October 11, 1863, and died.
McLeod, Donald M.		Accidentally killed.
Moore, Ed.	Apr. 30, 1862	Released by substitute, 1862.
Norwell, George T.	Apr. 30, 1862	Absent on surgeon's certificate October 30, 1862. Killed at Barrow's Shop, near Harrisburg, July 13, 1864.
Nelson, Thomas E.		Absent, sick, May 11, 1864.
Neeley, Charles		Killed at Brice's Cross Roads June 10, 1864.
Odell, S. K.		Transferred from Company F August 27, 1862. Detailed as forage master February 3, 1862.
Owen, Thomas P.	Apr. 30, 1862	April 30, 1862, left in Tennessee. Dismounted May, 1864.
Pope, E. F.	Aug. 1, 1863	Orderly to Col. Duckworth February 29, 1864.
Peebles, L. B.	Apr. 30, 1864	Detailed as courier for Gen. Villipigue, 1862.

Rooks, George W		
Rainey, A. L.		Wounded at Medon or Britton's Lane 1862. Absent on surgeon's certificate October 30, 1862. Rejoined April 1, 1864.
Robertson, J. H.		Wounded at Britton's Lane September 1, 1862.
Rice, D. P	Apr. 30, 1862	Transferred from Company L August 27, 1862.
Solomon, Henry	Apr. 30, 1862	Wounded at Hernando, 1862. Absent with surgeon's certificate October 30, 1862. Rejoined February 10, 1864. Wounded at Tishomingo Creek June 10, 1863; Harrisburg July 14, 1864.
Stewart, N.J	Apr. 30, 1862	Detailed as wagoner, 1862. Wounded near Prairie Mound, Miss., February 29, 1864.
Sheppard, Egbert H.		Color-sergeant. Wounded at Collierville October 11, 1866; Harrisburg July 11, 1864.
Scott, W. M.		
Sangster, John	Apr. 1, 1864	Absent without leave May 11, 1864.
Smith, James H.		Wounded at Tishomingo Creek June 10, 1864.
Smith, A. F.		
Smith, Joseph E.	Apr. 30, 1862	Absent on surgeon's certificate October 30, 1862.
Steele, William P	Apr. 30, 1862	Detailed as bugler August 1, 1862.
Sangster, H. C.		
Sutton, William J		
Sutton, J. Benjamin	Apr. 30, 1862	Died in service July 18, 1862.
Swan, Samuel H.		
Sheriff, John W		Captured at Oxford Dec. 2, 1862. Died in prison at Alton, Ill.
Stewart, N. J.		Detailed as wagoner October 30, 1862.
Stewart, William		
Sutton, William T.	Apr. 30, 1862	Rejoined April 1, 1864.
Sommerville, Jimmie		Killed at Brice's Cross Roads June 10, 1864.
Taliaferro, C. P	Apr. 30, 1862	Released by substitute October, 1862.
Transon, E. T	Apr. 4, 1862	Absent with leave February 29, 1864. Absent, sick, May 11, 1864.

Name.	Date of Enlistment.	Remarks.
Transon, David		Discharged in 1862.
Taliaferro, R. E.		Transferred from Company D. Absent, sick, without leave February 29, 1864.
Thomas, J. A	Apr. 30, 1862	Rejoined April 1, 1864.
Thomas, A. J		Died in service, 1864.
Tanner, L.	Apr. 1, 1864	Absent on surgeon's certificate May 11, 1864.
Taylor, S. A.		
Taylor, Frank M	Apr. 1, 1864	Discharged second time, sick, May, 1864.
Trail, W. C		
Tarver, Mike.		
Tadlock, William		
Taliaferro, D. C.		Died in hospital at Grenada September 1, 1863. Captured at Britton's Lane September 1, 1862. Absent without leave October 30, 1862.
Taliaferro, Vernon		
Tugwell, John	Apr. 30, 1862	Died June 1, 1862.
White, John B		
White, R. T.		
Wateradge, D H.	Apr. 30, 1862	Rejoined April 1, 1864.
Wateradge, Daniel.		
Wilson, J. M.		
Whitmore, Ed.	Aug. 1, 1862	Absent, sick, since January 13, 1862.
Witherspoon, H. H.		
Willis, Henry B.	Apr. 30, 1862	Killed Feb. 21, 1864, near Prairie Mound, and buried at Okolona. Absent on surgeon's certificate October 30, 1862. Discharged, sick, and died during war.
Williams, Solomon		
Witherspoon, Wm.	Apr. 4, 1862	Transferred from Company I, 1862. Ordered to duty as brevet second lieutenant January 13, 1864.

The Seventh Tennessee Calvary.   223

Colored Men with Company L.

Alison, Sam
Byers, Bill
Claiborne, Henry
Colbert, Ed

Curry, Jim
Moore, Joe
Nelson, Joe
Pugh, Dawson

O'Dell, Stephen
Pugh, Jeff
Taliaferro, Delynn

Taylor, George
Taylor, Hack
Taylor, Dick

Company M.

Name	Rank.	Date of Enlistment.	Remarks.
James G. Haywood	Captain.		Absent with leave October 30, 1862.
Benjamin T. Davis	Captain.		Absent without leave December 31, 1863. February 29, 1864, in parole camp.
J. M. Shaw	Lieutenant.		Released on certificate of discharge
W. H. Moore	Lieutenant.		Absent without leave December 31, 1863. In parole camp February 29, 1864.
C. S. O. Rice	Lieutenant.		Paroled December 31, 1863.
J. L. Livingston	Lieutenant.		On duty with regiment April 30, 1864.
J. H. Mann	Sergeant.	Apr. 16, 1862	Appointed Second Sergeant July 16, 1862; and First Sergeant December 1, 1862.
J. T. Green	Sergeant.	June 12, 1862	Appointed Third Sergeant October 23, 1862. Detailed as clerk at Pemberton's head-quarters December 31, 1862. Absent without leave April 30, 1864.
H. W. Keller	Sergeant.	Apr. 16, 1862	On special duty at head-quarters October 30, 1862. Absent without leave December 31, 1862, and February 29, 1864.
John Haywood	Sergeant.	May 12, 1862	Appointed Corporal September 20, 1862; First Corporal July 1, 1862. Absent without leave December 31, 1862. In prison February 29, 1864.

Name.	Rank.	Date of Enlistment.	Remarks.
T. A. Walker	Sergeant	Apr. 16, 1862	Absent, sick or captured while on detached duty December 31, 1862.
G. W. Young	Sergeant		Wounded at Columbia, Tenn., November 25, 1864.
N. A. Currie	Sergeant		
T. C. Anthony	Corporal	Apr. 16, 1862	On detached duty December 31, 1863.
J. D Greaves	Corporal	Apr. 16, 1862	Appointed Corporal September 4, 1862. Wounded at Harrisburg July 14, 1864.
S. Moore	Corporal	Apr. 16, 1862	Appointed Corporal October 1, 1862.

Privates.

Name.	Date of Enlistment.	Remarks.
Batchelor, James	May 23, 1862	Captured October 10, 1862, near Hatchie River, and paroled.
Borum, J. W	Apr. 16, 1862	Paroled December 31, 1863. Absent without leave June 30, 1864.
Blackwell, Joseph	Apr. 16, 1862	Absent without leave December 31, 1864.
Barns, T. W	Apr. 16, 1862	Absent without leave December 6, 1863.
Borum, B. S.		
Burks, J. D.		
Braden, Reuben		Killed at Harrisburg, July 14, 1864.
Bowers, T. W	Apr. 16, 1862	Absent without leave February 29, 1864.
Borum, T. W	Apr. 16, 1862	Absent without leave June 30, 1864.
Cunningham, J. C	Apr. 16, 1862	Captured July 10, 1862, in Haywood County, and paroled.
Claiborne, W B	Apr. 16, 1862	Discharged September 15, 1862 (Second Sergeant).
Currie, N. A	Apr. 16, 1862	Special duty at head-quarters October 30, 1862.
Cobb, John	Sept. 16, 1862	Absent without leave December 31, 1862. Paroled Feb. 29, 1864.
Curlin, J. W	Apr. 26, 1862	Special duty at head-quarters October 27, 1862.
Clark, John A		

The Seventh Tennessee Calvary.   225

Castello, J. N.		
Currie, T.....		
Carlton, A. M		
Cobb, William		
Currie, Jesse		Died at home
Coker, James		
Curtis, J. W...		
Carrigan, Jimmie		
Dean, George...		
Dunlap, J. B.	Sept. 15, 1862	Wounded at Harrisburg July 11, 1864.
Denny, Henry.	Apr. 16, 1862	Absent without leave December 31, 1861.
Dickerson, J. V.	Apr. 16, 1862	Absent without leave December 7, 1862, to April 15, 1864. Re-joined April 15, 1864.
Dickerson, J.	Apr. 16, 1862	Deserted December 1, 1862, at Abbeville, Miss
Durham, M	Aug. 24, 1864	Absent without leave Oct. 30, 1862. On detached duty Dec 31, 1862. Paroled December 31, 1863.
Davis, R. B.		
Fowlkes, J. Hick		
Fitzhugh, J. F		
Gause, J. P	Apr. 15, 1862	Wounded at Medon or Britton's Lane, 1862. Substituted for T. G. Gause July 1, 1862. Absent without leave December 31, 1863. Wounded at Harrisburg July 11, 1864.
Gause, T. G		
Gravitt, E. R..	Apr. 15, 1862	Absent without leave December 31, 1862.
Gause, J. L.	Apr. 15, 1862	Absent without leave February 29, 1864.
Green, J. M.		Killed at Britton's Lane September 1, 1862.
Gregory, Bascom G	Apr. 16, 1862	Discharged July 16, 1862.
Green, Milton	Apr. 16, 1862	Killed at Britton's Lane September 1, 1862.
Green, Taswell		
Gibbs, Samuel....		

Name.	Date of Enlistment.	Remarks.
Greaves, J. D		Wounded at Harrisburg July 14, 1864.
Harbert, J. H.	Apr. 16, 1862	Killed July 20, 1862, near Hatchie River, and paroled.
Hunter, H. A.	Apr. 16, 1862	Killed at Britton's Lane September 1, 1862.
Henderson, W. A.	Apr. 16, 1865	Discharged July 15, 1862.
Hancock, G. B.	Apr. 15, 1862	Absent without leave December 31, 1862.
Hastings, William		Wounded, captured, and died in prison, 1863.
Harris, James		Wounded at Tishomingo Creek, Miss., June 10, 1864.
Henfren, William A.		Discharged July 15, 1862, at Coldwater.
Haskins, E. T	Apr. 30, 1862	Died August 28, 1863, in St. John's Hospital, New Orleans
Jayrol, A. B.	Apr. 16, 1862	Absent without leave December 31, 1863. Paroled February 29, 1864.
Johnson, R. F.		Discharged July 15, 1862.
Killer, Hiram S		
Lackey, J. A.		
Lake, T. E.		
Lake, William	Apr. 16, 1862	Captured July 28, 1862. Exchanged September 27, 1862. Sick October 30, 1862. Rejoined April 15, 1864.
Mann, A. S		
Mann, Joel		Substitute for J. E. Macklin September 21, 1862.
Macklin, James S.		
McDougall, E. M		
Moses, Thomas J		
Maclin, J. F	Apr. 16, 1862	Discharged September 21, 1862.
Nevell, J. B.	June 2, 1862	Absent without leave from August 25, 1863, to May 12, 1864. In parole camp.
Neighbors, Lafayette		Died in prison.
Neighbors, J. P	Apr. 16, 1862	Captured July 29, 1862, on Hatchie River. Exchanged September 27, 1862. Died at Ripley, Tenn, November 15, 1862.

Name	Date	Remarks
Oldham, E. R.	Apr. 16, 1862	Paroled December 31, 1863. Absent without leave June 30, 1864.
Oldham, Sydney		Wounded at Harrisburg, Miss., July 14, 1864.
Pennington, W. B.	Apr. 16, 1862	Absent. Said to be captured and paroled October 30, 1862.
Powers, J. L.		
Pope, David P.	Feb. 4, 1862	Absent without leave Dec. 31, 1863. In parole camp Feb. 29, 1864.
Rainey, P. C.	Apr. 16, 1862	Absent without leave Dec. 31, 1863. In parole camp Feb. 19, 1864.
Rainey, T. C.		
Reed, H. T.	Apr. 16, 1862	Discharged August 29, 1862.
Rice, D. J.	Apr. 16, 1862	Absent, sick, October 30, 1862. Absent without leave April 30, 1864.
Rice, E. S. O.		
Rose, A.	Apr. 16, 1862	Discharged July 15, 1862.
Rice, Thomas S.		Killed at Tishomingo Creek, Miss., June 10, 1864.
Rayner, William		Killed at Tishomingo Creek, Miss., June 10, 1864.
Rice, J. S.	Aug. 1, 1862	On duty with regiment June 30, 1864.
Shaw, Archer		Wounded at Nashville December 1, 1864.
Shaw, N. A.	Apr. 16, 1862	Absent without leave from June, 1863, to January 23, 1864. In parole camp February 29, 1864.
Smith, A. F.		
Smith, J. F.	Nov. 10, 1863	Transferred from Company I, Eleventh Tennessee Regiment, May 1, 1864.
Tatum, G. G.		
Tipton, P.	May 24, 1862	Absent without leave December 31, 1863.
Temples, John	Apr. 16, 1862	Absent without leave February 29, 1864.
Wilkins, Irie		
Walker, B. R.		
West, John		

Note.—The errors which may appear in the names and details in the foregoing rolls are due to contradictory entries on the muster rolls, many of which are irreconcilable.

www.ingramcontent.com/pod-product-compliance
Lightning Source LLC
Chambersburg PA
CBHW021815230426
43669CB00008B/755